Editorial Project Manager
Lori Kamola, M.S. Ed.

Editor-in-Chief
Sharon Coan, M.S. Ed.

Cover Artist
Wendy Roy

Art Coordinator
Denice Adorno

Imaging
James Edward Grace

Product Manager
Phil Garcia

Many pages taken from
Extension Activity Book Series,
Teaching Spice, and *Thinking*
Skills Series
Publisher:
Blake Education

P9-CBU-951

More Brain Puzzlers

Fun Thinking Games and Activities to be Done Independently

Ages 8–12

Contributing Authors

Rosalind Curtis, Maiya Edwards,
Jean Haack, Fay Holbert,
Sharon Shapiro, Timothy Tuck

Publishers
Rachelle Cracchiolo, M.S. Ed.
Mary Dupuy Smith, M.S. Ed.
Americanized Edition

Teacher Created Materials, Inc.
6421 Industry Way
Westminster, CA 92683
www.teachercreated.com
©2002 Teacher Created Materials, Inc.
Made in U.S.A.
ISBN-0-7439-3355-9

Table of Contents

Table of Contents *(cont.)*

Table of Contents *(cont.)*

Table of Contents *(cont.)*

Table of Contents *(cont.)*

Table of Contents *(cont.)*

Table of Contents *(cont.)*

Table of Contents (cont.)

Introduction

Today's children are the problem solvers of the future. Children need many opportunities to explore creative solutions to problems and, unfortunately, many activity books for children ask questions with only one right answer or that can be answered without much thought put into the process. This book is a compilation of creative, fun, and unique activities for children to complete independently. This book is divided into three sections, *Brain Warm-ups, Brain Workouts,* and *Brain Challenges,* progressing from easier activities to more challenging ones. Within each section are four categories: Math, Word Activities, Writing, and Creative Thinking. While the first three of these categories are often thought of as basic skills, in this book, the activities all emphasize creative thinking strategies. Some of the activity pages are word puzzles with a twist: each asks a question that is solved with the help of a clue or some scrambled letters after the rest of the activity has been completed. Other activities include math word problems that encourage drawing pictures to help solve the question. On other pages, children are given a creative writing prompt and encouraged to write and illustrate a story. Many pages are fun thinking skills activities asking children to create new objects or change and improve objects and explain their thinking. All children can learn to think more critically and creatively. A foundation in creative thinking skills will enable children to pursue lifelong learning.

What Is a Thinking Skill?

In addition to helping us think clearly, thinking skills help us critically and creatively collect information to effectively solve problems. As a result of learning thinking skills, children will also become more aware of decision-making processes.

Improved thinking encourages children to look at a variety of ideas, search to greater depth, practice more critical decision making, challenge accepted ideas, approach tasks in decisive ways, and search for misunderstandings, while keeping the aims of the task clearly in mind.

The end results will be decisions that are more reliable, deeper understanding of concepts, contributions that are more creative, content that is examined more critically, and products that are more carefully created.

Why Do Children Need to Develop Thinking Skills?

Children need to develop the abilities to judge, analyze, and think critically in order to function in a democratic and technological society. A family should value the development of thinking skills and provide opportunities for these processes to be modeled and developed. Thinking skills can be taught, and all students can improve their thinking abilities. Creativity is present in children regardless of age, race, socioeconomic status, or different learning modes.

The basic skills are generally thought of as reading, writing, spelling, and math. These processes involve computation, recall of facts, and the basic mechanics of writing. Of course, parents should want their children to master basic skills, but the learning process should not stop there. Frequently, children are faced with tasks that expect them to demonstrate their ability to use higher level thinking without having had the opportunities to develop their abilities with these thinking processes.

Introduction *(cont.)*

Thinking Domains

It is desirable to develop different thinking domains, as they have different aims and develop different skills:

♦ *Critical thinking* examines, clarifies, and evaluates an idea, belief, or action's reasonableness. Students need to *infer*, *generalize*, take a *point of view*, *hypothesize*, and find *temporary solutions*.

♦ *Brainstorming*, *linking ideas*, *using analogies*, *creating original ideas*, *organizing information*, and looking at a problem from *different perspectives* will lead to alternative solutions useful in decision making and problem solving.

♦ The *collection*, *retention*, *recall*, and *use of information* when needed is another vital skill.

♦ *Creative thinking* develops original ideas.

Thinking Processes

Eight processes, categorized into cognitive and affective abilities, have been identified as being important in fostering thinking skills:

Cognitive (thinking) Abilities

Fluency allows as many ideas as possible to be thought of by children.

Flexibility helps children look at problems from different perspectives and think of ways to combine unusual ideas into something new and different. At times, objects may have to be grouped according to different criteria.

Originality involves producing unusual or unique ideas.

Elaboration involves adding or further developing ideas.

Affective (feeling) Abilities

Curiosity involves working out an idea by instinctively following a pathway.

Complexity involves thinking of more complex ways of approaching a task. This may involve searching for links, looking for missing sections, or restructuring ideas.

Risk-taking is seen in children who guess and defend their ideas without fear that others will make fun of their thoughts.

Imaginative children can picture and instinctively create what has never occurred and imagine themselves in other times and places.

Introduction *(cont.)*

Parents can help their children learn thinking skills in a variety of ways. There are many questions that parents can ask of themselves:

☆ Do our children have opportunities to work on problems where creative thinking is valued?

☆ Are they encouraged to apply history's lessons to today's problems?

☆ Are they involved in planning family outings that will satisfy the needs of all family members?

☆ Are they allowed to participate in family projects such as redesigning rooms?

☆ Most importantly, are children allowed to be different?

☆ Are they listened to, even if their ideas are unusual or impractical?

☆ Are they reassured that, even if they are disagreed with, their ideas and input are valuable?

☆ In terms of the family as a whole, are they encouraged to be part of an environment where it is acceptable to make mistakes?

☆ Is the focus on learning from our children?

Introduction *(cont.)*

Computer skills can be integrated into many aspects of the learning experience. Computer technology is useful for programming and problem solving. Spreadsheets and databases can develop higher-order thinking skills and lateral thinking. They will also develop spatial orientation. Computer games can be used to motivate students and encourage task commitment. When software is carefully selected, it can be used to develop higher-order thinking skills. Simulation or strategy software is motivational and open-ended and involves players in critical thinking, risk taking, and real-life problem solving.

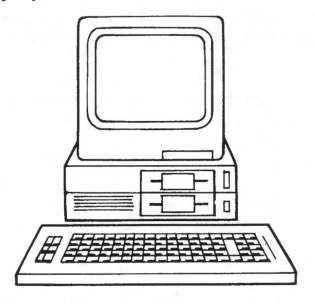

·························· **Assessment** ··························

Many pages in this book have open-ended answers; no one correct answer is required. For the pages with concrete answers, an answer key is provided at the back of the book. These pages are not meant to be graded; the answer key is provided for self-checking of answers. Many of the pages in this book ask thought-provoking questions, stimulating the children to think creatively and use their imaginations. Children can work on the activities at their own rate; a progress chart is included for children who like to keep track of the activities they have completed. A parent or other adult might choose to mark the progress chart with a sticker or a stamp after the activities have been completed to reward the child for a job well done. Also provided are some awards in the back of the book that parents can fill out and give when their children complete several of the activity pages. Children often enjoy devising their own problem-solving techniques; space is provided on the activity pages for children to explain how they arrived at their answers.

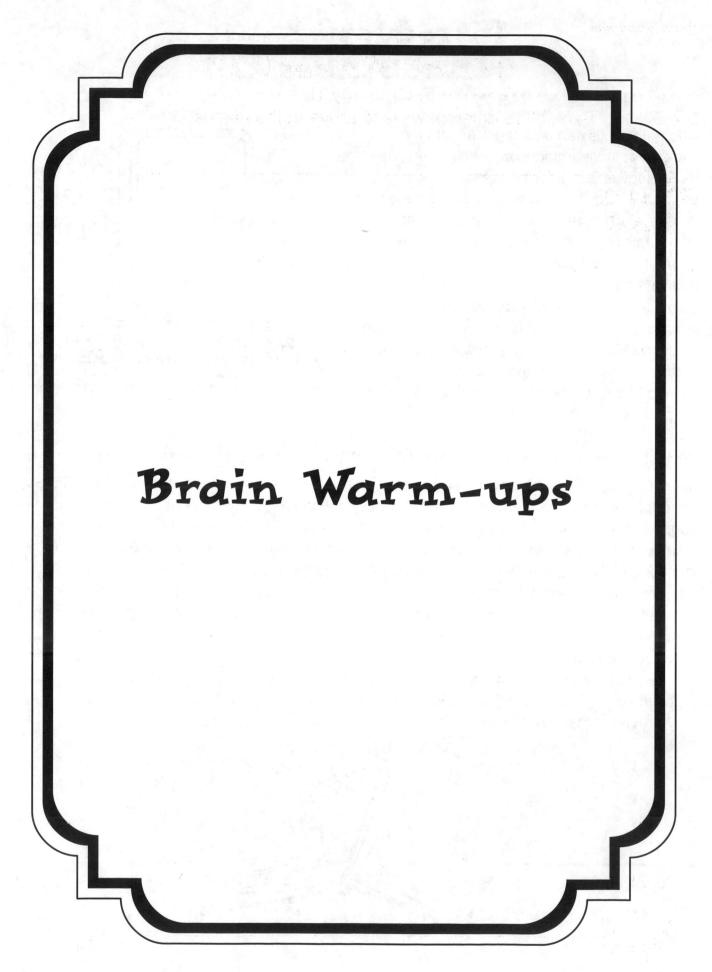

Brain Warm-ups

What Makes 12?

6 x 2 = 12. Think of 10 different ways to arrive at the number 12.

Patterns

Look at the patterns that have been started. Complete the patterns. The first row has been started for you. Trace over the dotted shapes and complete the rest of the page.

Standard Measurements

1. List the standard units of measurement that you know.

_____

_____

2. Write down some reasons why we need standard measurements.

_____

_____

3. What do you think people used before there were standard weights?

_____

_____

4. Write down some difficulties of using these different types of measurement.

_____

_____

_____

5. You have a two-pound and a three-pound weight. How will you measure the following amounts of bananas? (There may be more than one way.)

7 pounds	10 pounds
1 pound	20 pounds

Scaling Scales

Draw as many different types of scales as you can.

Invent your own weighing machine. It needs to be able to show objects that are heavier, lighter, or equal in weight. Draw and label your scales.

John, Jack, and the Nuggets

"This is tricky," said Jack to his friend John. "We've got 10 large nuggets of gold, and 11 smaller ones. How are we going to divide them up?"

"Well," said John. "What if I count clockwise around the circle and take each fifth nugget? When I've got 10, you can have the 11 that are left."

"That sounds pretty fair," replied Jack.

But it wasn't. John ended up with all 10 big nuggets. From where did he start counting?

Tortoise Trails

These four tortoises are trotting off to a juicy patch of grass. They're all waddling at the same speed, so which one will get there first? (Hint: You need to measure!)

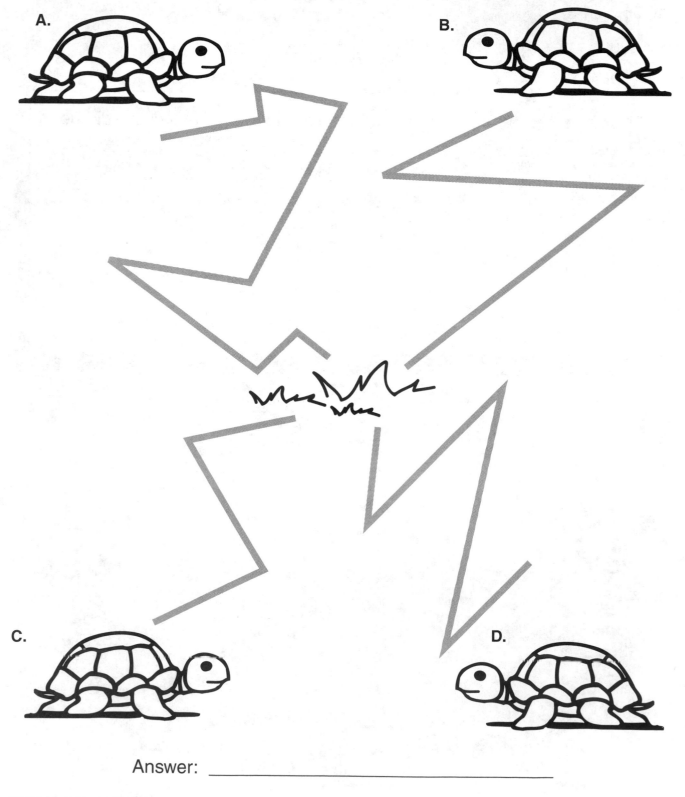

Answer: _____

House Math

What a house! It has thousands of windows, doors, floors, ceilings—very strange. It is almost as strange as the house that—that what? Read the written numbers. Then write the matching letter in the answer space. Read the answer vertically.

	Written Numbers	**Answer**
1	seven hundred fourteen	
2	two thousand four	
3	nine thousand, three hundred seven	
4	three hundred fifty-seven, doubled	
5	seventy-four	
6	ten thousand minus six hundred ninety-three	
7	six hundred twelve	
8	two thousand, four hundred eighty-one	
9	one hundred eleven	
10	nine hundred eight	
11	six thousand sixty-five	
12	two hundred forty-two	
13	one hundred two, times seven	

A	B	C	F	H	I	J	K	L	M	O	T	U
9307	111	612	8759	2004	6065	74	2481	242	3512	90	714	908

Invasion: Earth!

The Martians are invading! They're fed up with seeing themselves portrayed on Earth TV as horrible two-headed monsters (when actually they are horrible three-headed monsters), and they are out for revenge. They have filled up their spaceship tanks with gas and headed here as fast as they can. But will they make it? Their tanks only hold 50 million gallons of gas and Earth is . . . how far away is Earth? Follow the maze by adding the numbers to find the shortest distance to Earth.

Will they make it? _____

How far away is Earth? _____

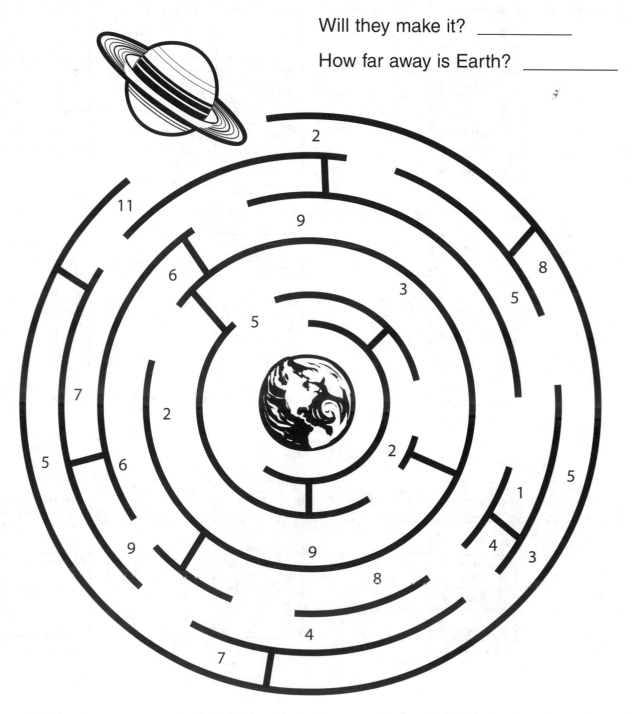

Door-to-Door

It's a hard life, selling door-to-door, especially when you are selling doors. Anyhow, here are nine doors. Start with the equation that has an answer of one, and end at the number nine, drawing a line from one to the next. Don't go to the wrong door at the wrong time—it could easily unhinge you . . . .

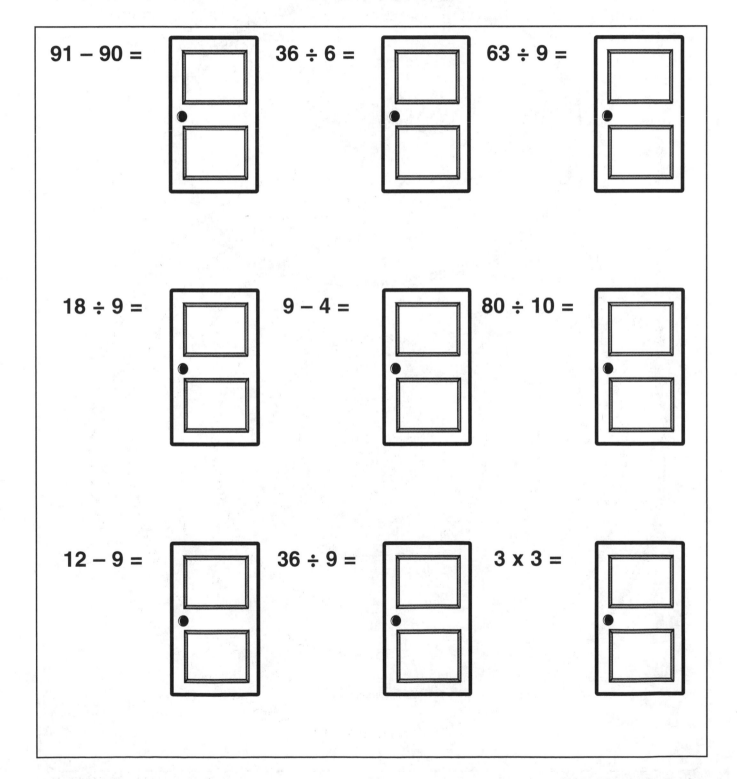

$91 - 90 =$

$36 \div 6 =$

$63 \div 9 =$

$18 \div 9 =$

$9 - 4 =$

$80 \div 10 =$

$12 - 9 =$

$36 \div 9 =$

$3 \times 3 =$

Doughnut Decision

There is only one doughnut, but there are eight people. Can you cut the doughnut into equal pieces, using only three cuts? Show your work.

Exam Time

As Mr. Teran prepared to pass back the last spelling exam, five anxious students awaited their grades. Using the clues below, determine each child's grade. Mark an **X** in each correct box.

1. Lucy, who did not get an A on her test, scored higher than Martin and Gwen.

2. Cara and Gwen both scored higher than Donald.

3. Martin received a C on his test.

4. No two students received the same grade.

	A	B	C	C-	D
Lucy					
Gwen					
Cara					
Martin					
Donald					

Proverbial Codes

Use this code to decode and finish the sentences.

Number	6	7	8	9	0	1	2	3	4	5	16	17	18
Code	A	B	C	D	E	F	G	H	I	J	K	L	M

Number	19	20	21	22	23	24	25	26	27	28	29	30	31
Code	N	O	P	Q	R	S	T	U	V	W	X	Y	Z

1. (17 20 20 16) _____ before you (17 0 6 21)

   _____.

2. Never put off until (25 20 18 20 23 23 20 28)

   _____ what can be done (25 20 9 6 30)

   _____.

3. A (1 23 4 0 19 9) _____ in (19 0 0 9)

   _____ is a (1 23 4 0 19 9) _____

   (4 19 9 0 0 9) _____.

4. The early (7 4 23 9) _____ catches the (28 20 23 18)

   _____.

5. All that (2 17 4 25 25 0 23 24) _____ is not (2 20 17 9)

   _____.

6. Don't (8 23 30) _____ over (24 21 4 17 17 0 9)

   _____ milk.

7. You never (16 19 20 28) _____ what you can do

   (26 19 25 4 17) _____ you (25 23 30) _____.

8. Make (30 20 26 23 24 0 17 1) _____ necessary to

   (24 20 18 0 20 19 0) _____.

Word Problems

Read each word problem and then answer the questions.

1. Daniel bought two candy bars at 47 cents each. How much did he spend?

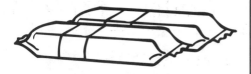

2. Laura had 92 cents. She wanted to buy a 35 cent juice and a 49 cent hot dog. How much did she spend? How much change does she receive?

3. Jim put his pennies into two small boxes. He put 1,396 pennies into each box. How many pennies did he have?

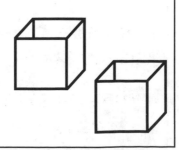

Word Problems *(cont.)*

Read each word problem and then answer the questions.

4. The Wilson's drove their car 10,483 miles one year and 19,768 miles the next year. How far did they drive during the two years?

5. Robyn had 296 marbles in one box and 187 marbles in another box. How many marbles did she have?

6. In 1959, the population of Happyville was 18,746. During the next 20 years, the population increased by 19,658. What was the population in 1979?

Word Problems *(cont.)*

Read each word problem and then answer the questions.

7. Russell bought four bags of chips at 60 cents each, two sodas at 35 cents each, and two cookies at 25 cents each. How much did he spend?

8. Tamara wanted to go bowling. She rented shoes for $10.00, paid for two games at $2.00 a game, and bought one soda for $.35. How much did she spend?

9. Kristen had 12 red socks, 27 green socks, 13 blue socks, and 32 pink socks. How many socks did she have?

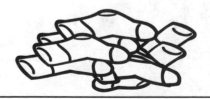

10. Paul has 75 rocks in his collection. His Uncle Joe has 139 and wants to give them to Paul. How many will he then have?

Time

Imagine that all the clocks have stopped. How many different ways can you invent to measure time?

Which one do you think would work best? Why?

Frog Hop!

Here are the results for the Calaveras County Frog Jumping Competition. The only question is, who won? Remember: the frog's score is the aggregate (total) of their jumps.

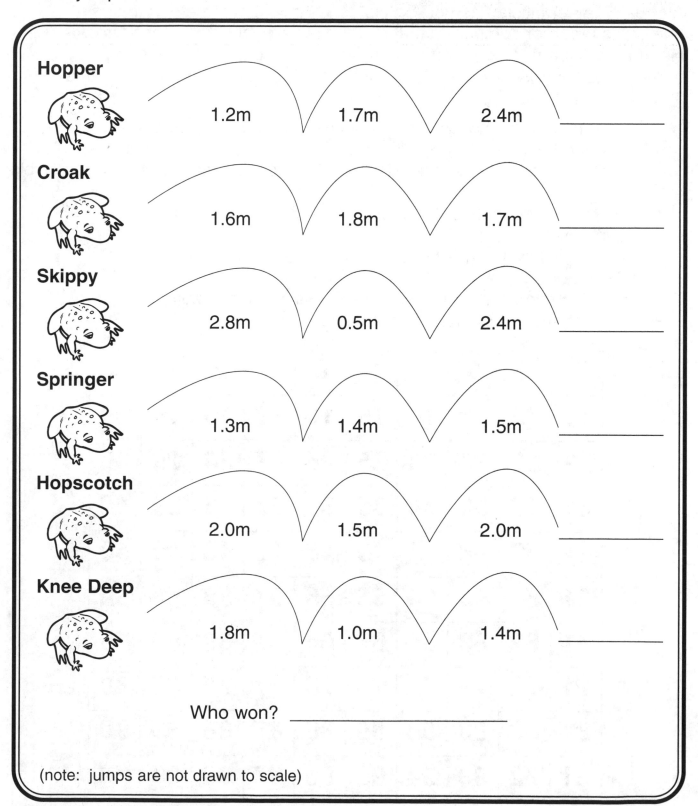

Hopper

1.2m   1.7m   2.4m   _____

Croak

1.6m   1.8m   1.7m   _____

Skippy

2.8m   0.5m   2.4m   _____

Springer

1.3m   1.4m   1.5m   _____

Hopscotch

2.0m   1.5m   2.0m   _____

Knee Deep

1.8m   1.0m   1.4m   _____

Who won? _____

(note: jumps are not drawn to scale)

Prime Time

Mathematicians put numbers into two categories—*prime* or *composite*. A *prime number* is a number with only two factors: one and itself. A *composite number* has more than two factors.

A Greek mathematician named Eratosthenes invented a method to see if a number is prime or composite; that method is called the *Sieve of Eratosthenes*. He arranged the numbers from 1 to 100 and used divisibility rules to find the prime numbers. Use the numbers in the box below and follow the steps to find the prime numbers.

- The number 1 is a special case. It is neither prime nor composite. Put a box around number 1.
- Number 2 is a prime number, so circle 2. Cross out all the numbers divisible by 2.
- Number 3 is a prime number, so circle 3. Then cross out all numbers divisible by 3.
- The next uncrossed number is 5. Circle 5 and then cross off all the multiples of 5.
- Circle 7. Seven is a prime number. Cross off all the multiples of 7.
- Any numbers that are left are prime, so circle them.

1	2	3	4	5	6	7	8	9	10
11	12	13	14	15	16	17	18	19	20
21	22	23	24	25	26	27	28	29	30
31	32	33	34	35	36	37	38	39	40
41	42	43	44	45	46	47	48	49	50
51	52	53	54	55	56	57	58	59	60
61	62	63	64	65	66	67	68	69	70
71	72	73	74	75	76	77	78	79	80
81	82	83	84	85	86	87	88	89	90
91	92	93	94	95	96	97	98	99	100

Word Stair Puzzle

Use the clues to fill in the grid.

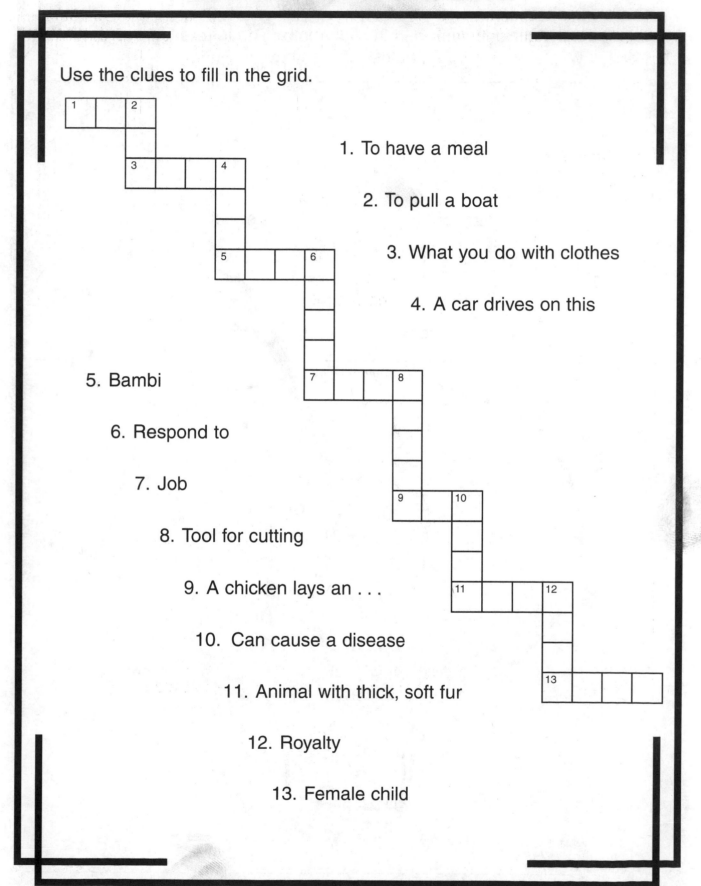

1. To have a meal

2. To pull a boat

3. What you do with clothes

4. A car drives on this

5. Bambi

6. Respond to

7. Job

8. Tool for cutting

9. A chicken lays an . . .

10. Can cause a disease

11. Animal with thick, soft fur

12. Royalty

13. Female child

Light Bulb Word Search

Find all of these light bulb words in the light bulb. The letters left over in the light bulb will tell you how many light bulbs you can buy.

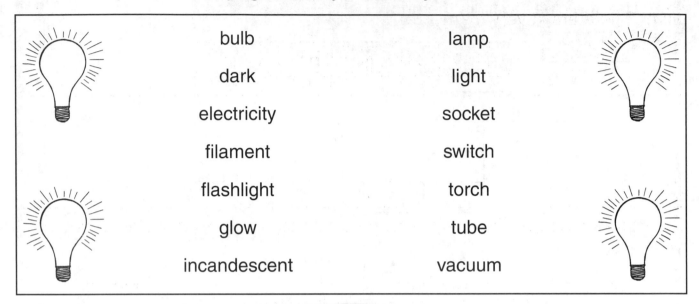

bulb	lamp
dark	light
electricity	socket
filament	switch
flashlight	torch
glow	tube
incandescent	vacuum

```
              I   E   T   T
          H   N   L   H   E   V
      O   E   C   E   G   K   A   L
  B   B   W   A   C   I   C   C   I   M
  U   A   H   N   T   L   O   U   G   N
T L H   C   D   R   H   S   U   H   Y   T
C B C   T   E   I   S   A   M   T   N   W
  N R   I   S   C   A   Y   O   E   O
  O W   C   I   L   U   M   L
  T S   E   T   F   A   G   A
      F   N   Y   L   K   F
          T   I   A   R
          F   O   M   A
          R   D   P   D
```

Answer: _____?

Keyboarding

How many five-letter words can you make using the middle row of the keyboard? You can only use each letter once.

(Hint: There aren't very many!)

The Dvorak keyboard (a special keyboard claimed to be much faster to type on) looks like this:

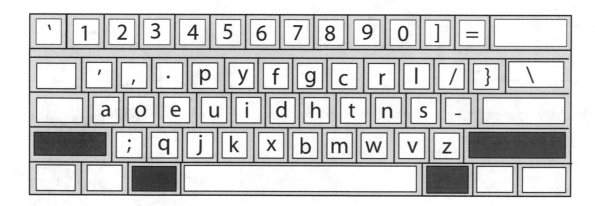

How many five-letter words can you make using the middle row of letters on this keyboard?

Pinocchio

Pinocchio was made from a magic piece of wood. How many words of three letters or more can you make out of the word "Pinocchio"?

P I N
O C C
H I O

_____   _____

_____   _____

_____   _____

_____   _____

_____   _____

_____   _____

_____   _____

_____   _____

_____   _____

Oyster Antics

Here is a bunch of oysters all sleeping in a shallow pool. Eight of them have pearls inside; the rest do not have pearls. To help you find the pearls, the oysters have labeled themselves. They have also arranged themselves into a helpful pattern. Find the pearls and circle the oysters with pearls. One has been circled for you. (Hint: What are pearls often made into? a _____)

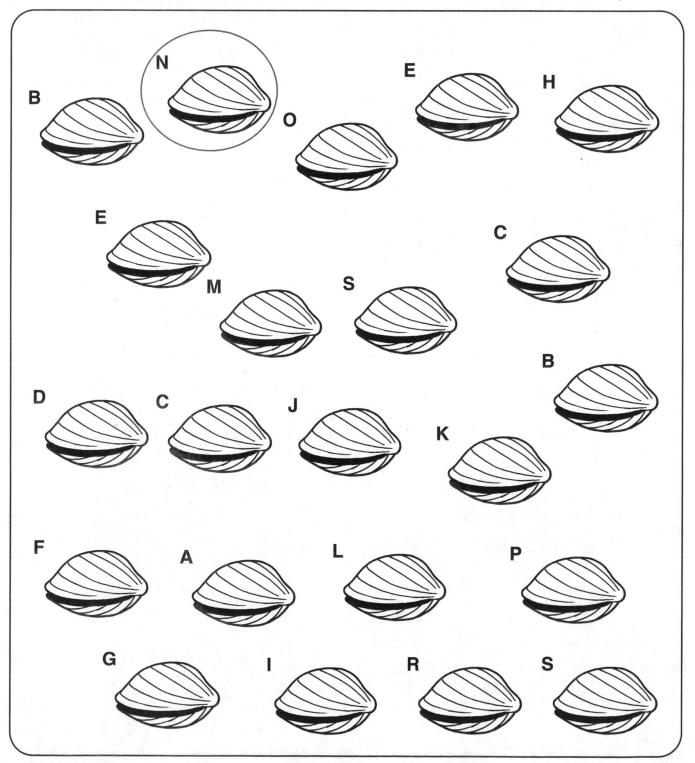

Word Twins

Some words just seem to fit together, like "day and night" or "bread and butter."
They are almost like twins! Below are two lists of 17 separated word twins.
Read the two lists of words and put the "twins" back together.

List 1		**List 2**	
aches	fish	again	paste
again	night	bolts	pepper
alive	nuts	cheese	pieces
bacon	odds	chips	roll
bells	rock	day	square
bits	salt	eggs	stripes
crackers	stars	ends	thin
cut	thick	kicking	whistles
fair		pains	

_____   _____

_____   _____

_____   _____

_____   _____

_____   _____

_____   _____

_____   _____

_____

Winnie-the-Pooh Word Puzzle

Solve the clues by using the letters of Winnie-the-Pooh's name as a guide.

1. Owl's spelling of his name

2. A bouncy tiger

3. A bouncy kangaroo

4. Winnie-the-Pooh sometimes went under this name

5. The entrance to this character's house seems smaller after eating honey.

6. A grumpy friend

7. Pooh Bear's best friend

8. Pooh Bear's favorite food

9. The characters live in the 100 _____ wood.

10. A small pig

11. A wise bird

12. Christopher's last name

13. How Rabbit spells house

Cornflake Word Chase

You might find snap, crackle, and pop in some cereals—but what can you find in a cornflake? How about more than 20 three-letter (or longer) words, all beginning with C!

Reading Scramble

Unscramble the letters to find words about books and reading.

1. ookb _____

2. brayrli _____

3. eard _____

4. sodrw _____

5. ictreup _____

6. tnpri _____

7. epga _____

8. rutaho _____

9. trtsai _____

10. etpy _____

11. ytrso _____

12. ptol _____

13. rcveo _____

14. cahatrcre _____

15. lusitariotnl _____

Alphabetical Order

Put the words in ABC order.

chain	yellow
table	drum
potato	egg
broom	flower
jar	whale
number	letter
star	hand
music	umbrella

1. _____

2. _____

3. _____

4. _____

5. _____

6. _____

7. _____

8. _____

9. _____

10. _____

11. _____

12. _____

13. _____

14. _____

15. _____

16. _____

Five-Letter Words

Each of the following words has a synonym that contains five letters. Write them on the lines.

1. big   __ __ r __ __

2. understand   __ __ __ __ n

3. tale   __ t __ __ __

4. correct   __ __ __ __ t

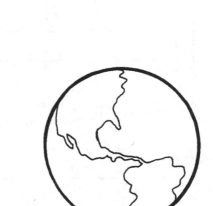

5. begin   s __ __ __ __

6. robber   __ __ i __ f

7. world   __ __ r __ __

8. cost   p __ __ __ __

9. record   __ r __ __ __

10. rush   __ __ r __ y

11. below   u __ __ __ __

12. permit   __ __ __ __ w

13. fetch   __ r __ __ __

14. glad   h __ __ __ __

15. yell   __ h __ __ __

The Great Outdoors

List words related to what you see outdoors. Write as many words as you can for each letter.

A _____

B _____

C _____

D _____

E _____

F _____

G _____

H _____

I _____

J _____

K _____

L _____

M _____

N _____

O _____

P _____

Q _____

R _____

S _____

T _____

U _____

V _____

W _____

X _____

Y _____

Z _____

Word Pairs

Write the missing half of each pair.

1. _____ and puff

2. _____ and feather

3. _____ and dogs

4. _____ and cranny

5. _____ and thin

6. _____ and match

7. _____ and nail

8. _____ and sugar

9. _____ and dandy

10. _____ and forth

11. _____ and holler

12. _____ and stones

13. _____ and down

14. _____ and cents

15. _____ and cream

16. _____ and order

17. _____ and fall

18. _____ and peace

19. _____ and out

20. _____ and white

21. _____ and proper

22. _____ and soul

23. _____ and satin

24. _____ and ladder

25. _____ and paper

What Did You See Today?

What did you see when you first woke up today? What did you see when you walked through the house? What did you see on your way to school? List everything you have seen today.

_____

_____

_____

_____

_____

_____

_____

_____

_____

_____

_____

Playing Games

Imagine an old tire. What does it look like? How heavy is it? How does it feel? How does it smell?

_____

_____

_____

_____

How many games can you make up using an old car tire?

_____

_____

_____

_____

If the tire was chopped into pieces, what could you use the different bits for? Remember that some bits of the tire are rough and some are smooth, and some have letters on them.

_____

_____

_____

_____

_____

The Pink Shirt

Your aunt has given you a pink shirt for your birthday, but you don't like the color pink. You don't want to hurt her feelings, but you don't want to wear it.

Write five good excuses why you can't wear the shirt.

1. _____

2. _____

3. _____

4. _____

5. _____

Write five ways that you could use the shirt instead of wearing it.

1. _____

2. _____

3. _____

4. _____

5. _____

Tennis, Anyone?

Write at least 10 uses for a tennis ball. They can be as silly as you like.

1. _____

2. _____

3. _____

4. _____

5. _____

6. _____

7. _____

8. _____

9. _____

10. _____

bonus _____

bonus _____

Is It a Ghost?

Write down all the things that this cloud looks like.

_____

_____

_____

_____

_____

_____

_____

All About Me

Make a little cartoon about yourself. The title is:

My Favorite Things to Do Every Day

1.	2.	3.
4.	5.	6.
7.	8.	9.

What a Hero!

Invent a story which tells about a heroic act by a tightrope-walker.

_____

_____

_____

_____

_____

_____

_____

_____

_____

_____

_____

_____

_____

Road Rules

What changes would you recommend to the current road rules to prevent traffic accidents?

Future Travel

Predict how students will travel to school in the future.

_____

_____

_____

_____

_____

_____

_____

_____

_____

_____

_____

_____

No Cars?

What would happen if there were no more cars in the world?

_____

_____

_____

_____

_____

_____

_____

_____

_____

_____

_____

_____

_____

The Handy Dandy Fairy Tale Writer

Use our Handy Dandy Fairy Tale Writer to construct your next fairy tale! Just take a main character from column one and a second one from column two, add in a location from column three, add a problem from column four, and a solution from five. Bingo! A brand new fairy tale!

1. _____ +
2. _____ +
3. _____ +
4. _____ =
5. _____

There are also five real fairy tales. Can you name them?

1. _____
2. _____
3. _____
4. _____
5. _____

Main Character One	Main Character Two	Location	Problem	Solution
A wolf	Large, smelly goat	Bridge	Collecting straw-into-gold-weaving debt	Blow down house
Another wolf	Selfish girl	Castle in the air	Collecting trolls	Dress up as grandmother
Elf with unusual name	Spoiled girl	Dark wood	Fending off starvation	Grind bones to make bread
Giant	Uncooperative pig	Dungeon	Finding pork	Take first born child
Troll	Young lout	House of bricks	Keeping Englishman out	Wait for bigger brother to come along

A Talking Shark

If you met a shark that could talk, what questions would you ask it?

_____

_____

_____

_____

_____

_____

_____

_____

_____

_____

_____

_____

_____

_____

You Ask the Questions

The answer is "a rose." Write at least three questions.

_____

_____

_____

_____

_____

_____

_____

The answer is "in the middle of the night." Write at least three questions.

_____

_____

_____

_____

_____

_____

_____

Recycle

What could you do with . . .

felt-tip pens that don't write anymore?

_____

_____

_____

a trampoline that has lost its bounce?

_____

_____

_____

cereal that has gone stale?

_____

_____

_____

It doesn't matter how silly the ideas are. Think of as many as you can.

Predicting the Future

What do you think children will wear to school 100 years in the future?

_____

_____

_____

_____

_____

What do you think you will be doing, and where will you be, in twenty years?

_____

_____

_____

_____

_____

How will you travel to school in the future?

_____

_____

_____

_____

_____

It Won't Happen!

Name 10 things you can't hear.

Name five people you will never meet.

Name seven things that can't be photographed.

Brainstorm!

There are no right or wrong answers, so be creative.

Name all the things that you can think of that move.

_____

_____

_____

_____

What are things that are found underground? List as many as you can.

_____

_____

_____

List everything that you can think of that is pink.

_____

_____

_____

_____

Redesign Your Object

Choose an object that you could redesign. It could be a spade, or a kitchen utensil, such as tongs, a colander, a whisk, a spoon or fork, or anything else that you choose.

Describe what the object is used for.

_____

_____

_____

Brainstorm other uses.

_____

_____

_____

Imagine that the object was re-made a hundred times larger. What uses would it have now?

_____

_____

_____

Choose one part of the object to change. List its new uses.

_____

_____

_____

Reverse or rearrange part of the object. Draw what it looks like now.

The Evolving Classroom

Brainstorm ways that the classroom could be made a more comfortable, exciting, and interesting place.

Choose one of the possible changes and think of what would need to be done to make the change.

BÁR

> **B** stands for bigger
>
> **A** stands for add on
>
> **R** stands for replace/rearrange/change

Example: Draw a shoe

Ask what could be made **bigger**. For example, the sole of the shoe could be a platform three feet high, so that the wearer can see over people's heads in a crowd.

Add wings or a motor, to go places fast.

Replace the laces with snaps to make it easier to get the shoes off.

> Use the BAR process using your pencil as the object, giving reasons for each change. Silly and innovative ideas are encouraged.

What Is That?

Make up a new and strange animal and draw it here.

What is it called?

_____

Where does it live?

_____

What does it eat?

_____

Do You Want a Ride?

How many different things can you ride?

_____

_____

_____

_____

_____

_____

List all the things that you can push.

_____

_____

_____

_____

_____

_____

The Old Fire Engine

This fire engine is too old to be used as a fire engine anymore. It is going to be broken down into pieces. What could all the pieces be used for?

wheels _____

_____

ladder _____

_____

headlights _____

_____

seats _____

_____

steering wheel_____

_____

windshield _____

_____

hose _____

_____

other pieces _____

_____

What a Face!

Divide these faces into groups.

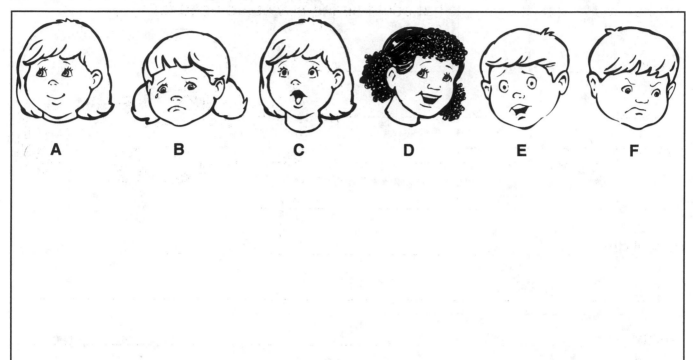

Explain your reasons for each group.

_____

_____

_____

_____

_____

_____

_____

Join the Pictures

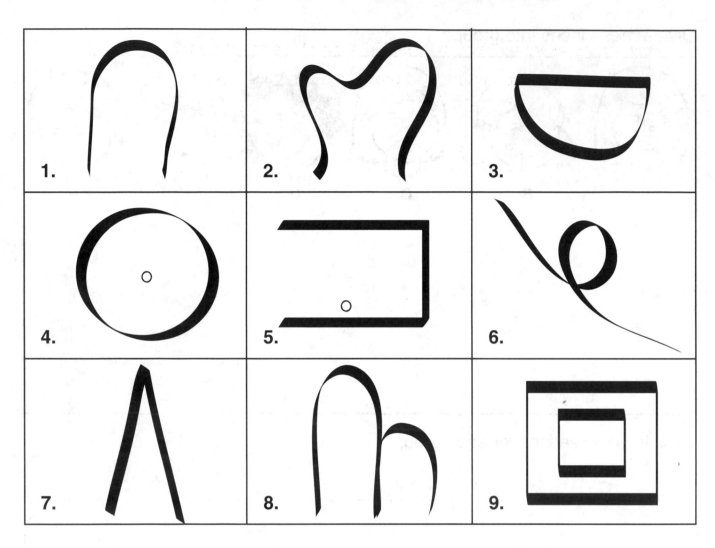

1. If picture one is a finger, what is picture four?_____

2. If picture seven is a mountain, what is picture six? _____

3. If picture two is a tooth, what is picture three? _____

4. If picture eight is a kennel, what is picture nine?_____

5. If picture four is a hat (you are looking down on it), what is picture five?

   _____

6. If picture eight is an Igloo, what is picture four? _____

7. If picture eight shows two rocks, what is picture one? _____

8. If picture five is a door (turn the page sideways), what do you see when you open the door at picture nine?_____

Travel

How many ways can you travel from one place to another?

List all the ways you know and draw pictures for each.

Talking About Birds

Ducks, geese, turkeys, and chickens are all domestic birds called fowls. They can all fly a bit, and some fly better than others.

1. In the table, rank these birds from worst to best flyers:

Worst Flyer	Okay Flyer	Better Flyer	Best Flyer

2. Why are ducks and geese able to swim, but turkeys and chickens are not? Illustrate your answer.

Movement

1. Write down four reasons why animals need to move.

   a. _____   c. _____

   b. _____   d. _____

2. Choose three animals and fill in the table to show some of the ways each one moves.

Animal	Method 1	Method 2	Method 3

3. Of your three animals, draw the fast movers on the left and the slow movers on the right.

Fast Movers	Slow Movers

4. Invent a creature that would be the best mover ever. Draw and label your "pet" to show the special purposes for the special parts.

Sundials

1. Draw some instruments that have been used to measure time.

2. Draw a sundial below and describe what it will be made from.

My sundial will look like this:

                                            My sundial is made from:

3. Explain how sundials work.

4. Where would be the best place to put your sundial on the playground? Explain why you chose that location.

Bicycles and Things

1. The first bicycle was built in England over 350 years ago. It had no pedals, and riders had to push it along with their feet! Draw this invention.

Bicycle from the year 1642

2. Now think about a 21st century "personal transport machine."

   How would it move? _____

   What would it be made of? _____

   What would it look like? _____

   Draw your invention here.

Personal Transport Machine for the year 2042

A Different Dog Kennel

Draw a dog kennel.

Can you make it different by:

making one part bigger?   adding something extra?

replacing one part with something else?

Not a Good Pet!

List animals which would not make good pets.

_____

_____

_____

_____

Why did you choose these animals?

_____

_____

_____

Draw pictures of three of the animals from your list.

Extinct Animals

Name five animals that are extinct.

1. _____

2. _____

3. _____

4. _____

5. _____

What are five questions you would liked to have asked one of the extinct animals?

1. _____

2. _____

3. _____

4. _____

5. _____

Draw pictures of all five animals.

The Circus

How many circus words can you think of in two minutes?

List all the people associated with the circus. Remember that there are many behind-the-scenes people, such as those who look after the animals, those who make the costumes, and those who sell food and tickets.

Separate the list of circus people into different categories such as funny acts, dangerous acts, etc.

A Different Kind of House

What would our houses look like if they had no corners?

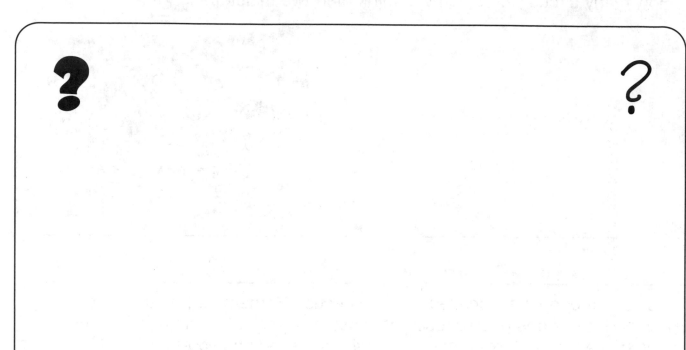

Spot the Forgery

Look at the two pictures—the one on the left is the original, the one on the right is a forgery. How many differences can you find between the two?

List the differences here:

Railway Words

Look carefully at these four word puzzles. Can you work out what each says?

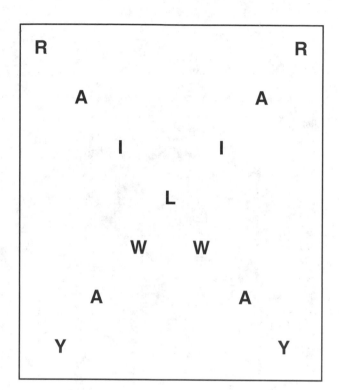

RAILWAY RAILWAY RAILWAY RAILWAY RAILWAY RAILWAY RAILWAY RAILWAY RAILWAY RAILWAY RAILWAY RAILWAY

Pipeline Puzzle

All those pipes, and so many in need of repair! So, the water goes in at the
arrow—and where does it come out?_____

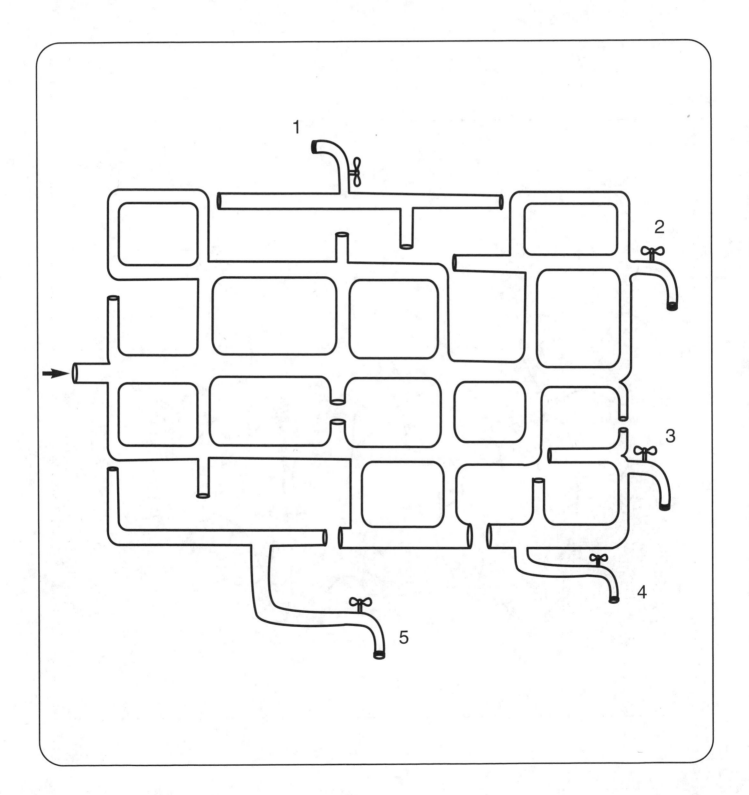

To Bee or Not to Bee . . .

This bee is confused. Its mate has just done a stunning dance to communicate exactly where the pollen is, but it got confused. Follow the trail and see where the bee ends up.

Lightning Rod

Benjamin Franklin was one of the first scientists to conclusively prove that lightning is a form of electricity. He achieved this by flying a kite in a thunderstorm. Later he tried it again, but with four kites. Unfortunately, he's only holding onto one of them. Two of the other kites are attached to each other, and the fourth is flying free. So, which kites are doing what?

A: _____

B: _____

C: _____

D: _____

Amazing!

Here's an April Fool's maze. Can you find your way from "in" to "out"?

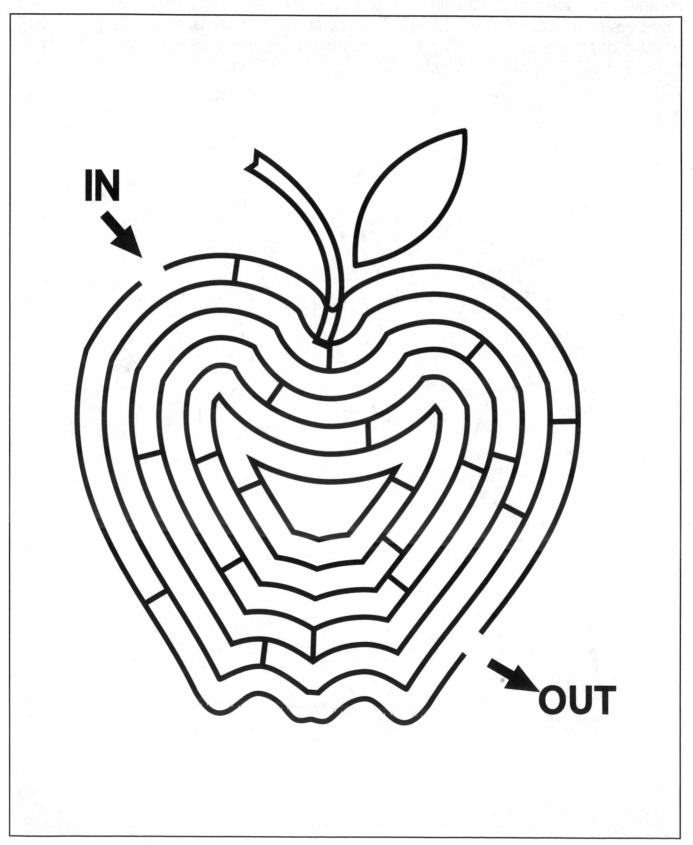

Colorful Language

Don't get the blues—get colorful! Complete each of these sentences with a color.

1. Don't run so fast—you're going _____ in the face!

2. You coward! You're just _____ !

3. Wait until Josh sees my new bike, he'll be _____ with envy.

4. Oh dear, you've gone as _____ as a ghost!

5. Watch out! The captain's face is _____ as thunder!

6. Everything's wonderful! We're in the _____ !

7. The whole show lost money. The books are way in the _____ .

8. Fetch an _____ from the fruit bowl please.

Assembly Line Blues

Unlike the car in the circle, the other five cars below have defects. The assembly line quality control supervisor spotted them. Can you?

A. _____

B. _____

C. _____

D. _____

E. _____

How Amazing!

Follow the maze to get the car in the garage.

Homes

Three children live on the same street. Each of their houses is a different color.
Can you use the clues to match each child to his or her house? Draw a line
between each child and home. Color the houses when you are through.

---

1. Marla's house is the color of cotton candy.

2. Pepper's house is the color of some apples.

3. Rosa's house is the color of corn on the cob.

Marla

Red House

Pepper

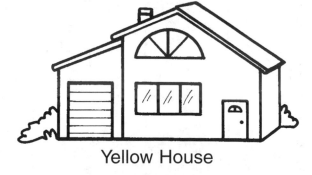

Yellow House

Rosa

Pink House

In the Library

Draw a picture of a library with the following in it:

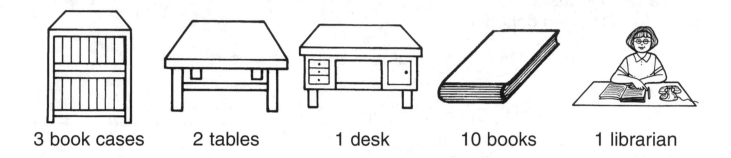

3 book cases   2 tables   1 desk   10 books   1 librarian

Which One Does Not Belong?

In each line below, one of the four words does not belong with the other three. Circle the one that does not fit. Explain what the others have in common. An example has been done for you.

relish, (hot dogs,) mustard, ketchup = condiments

1. October, November, December, June _____

2. boot, shoe, glove, slipper _____

3. notebook, pencil, pen, crayon _____

4. king, queen, prince, page _____

5. Bob, Robert, Rich, Robby _____

6. ebony, mahogany, carnation, cherry _____

7. chocolate chip, ginger snap, layer cake, animal cookie _____

8. girl, lass, nephew, woman _____

9. tape recorder, television, telephone, microphone _____

10. table, chair, sofa, flower _____

11. cantaloupe, casaba, grapefruit, watermelon _____

12. strange, thud, cry, hiss _____

13. cougar, jaguar, lion, elephant _____

14. hammer, screwdriver, drill, lightbulb _____

15. exclamation mark, question mark, colon, period _____

All Alike

Read the words on each line. Explain how they are alike. An example has been done for you.

north, south, east = cardinal directions

1. jazz, tap, ballet _____

2. tennis, soccer, basketball _____

3. lily, daffodil, gardenia _____

4. tiger, lion, jaguar _____

5. cookies, candy, ice cream _____

6. wrench, drill, hammer _____

7. mad, silly, grumpy _____

8. diamond, ruby, amethyst _____

9. milk, butter, cheese _____

10. single, alone, individual _____

11. orange, tennis ball, marble _____

12. plane, blimp, helicopter _____

13. pencil, pen, marker _____

14. Helena, Hillary, Heather _____

15. pumpkin, zucchini, acorn _____

Categorizing

In the word box below are 42 words, each of which belongs in one of the six categories—wood, metals, water, space, colors, and furniture. Place each of the words under the correct category. For example, **bay** would belong in the water category. Seven words belong under each category.

• bay	• oak	• chest	• river	• chartreuse
• Mars	• lake	• pond	• beige	• aluminum
• rocket	• ocean	• orbit	• copper	• weightless
• creek	• dresser	• board	• iron	• countdown
• sea	• tan	• cabinet	• forest	• pencil
• lamp	• scarlet	• couch	• titanium	• maple
• lumber	• platinum	• steel	• rocker	
• tin	• red	• blue	• walnut	
• mirror	• moon	• green	• astronaut	

Wood
_____
_____
_____
_____
_____
_____
_____

Metals
_____
_____
_____
_____
_____
_____
_____

Water
_____
_____
_____
_____
_____
_____
_____

Space
_____
_____
_____
_____
_____
_____
_____

Colors
_____
_____
_____
_____
_____
_____
_____

Furniture
_____
_____
_____
_____
_____
_____
_____

How Is Your Memory?

Study the picture for three minutes. Then, turn the page and write down as many items from the picture as you can remember.

How is Your Memory? *(cont.)*

New Products

Brainstorm ideas for each list.

Different types of clothing	Different modes of transportation
_____	_____
_____	_____
_____	_____
_____	_____
_____	_____

With your eyes closed, select one object from each list. Combine them to form a new object. Sketch and name the combined idea.	How would this new product affect your life? Describe what it could do.

My New Invention!

Use this shape as the basis for a new invention.

Draw the invention. Write its name on the line below your drawing.

_____

What is it used for?

_____

_____

_____

Family Categories

Draw a chart to show all the ways in which your family members can be categorized, for example, by size, weight, gender, interests. Can you think of 10 different categories?

Brain Workouts

School Days

Complete this pie graph to show how you spend your day at school. Show all your subjects, lunch and recess breaks, and the amount of time each one takes.

Your Ideal Day

Draw a pie graph showing how your ideal day would be spent.

Number Trivia

Imagine you are a contestant on the television quiz show called Number Trivia. How will you score?

1. What numbers are inferred by these words?

   Gross   _____   Binoculars   _____

   Octopus   _____   Unicorn   _____

   Centipede   _____

2. Which country has these currencies?

   Baht   _____   Pound   _____

   Lira   _____   Rupee   _____

   Yen   _____

3. In a garden there are 20 flowers. Seven are roses, eight are carnations, and five are daisies. If the garden had 28 roses, there would be _____ carnations, _____ daisies, and _____ flowers altogether.

4. Five athletes competed in the 100 meter sprint. The athlete from Canada won. The athlete from Mexico came last. The athlete from Australia was ahead of the athlete from South Africa and just behind the athlete from the United States.

   Who came in second? _____

5. Here is an example of one way to plant five trees in two rows so that each row contains three trees. Can you think of another way?

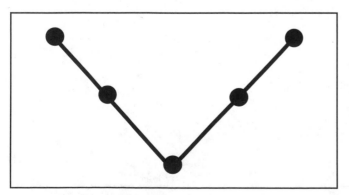

Rearrange the Numbers

Rearrange the numbers below so that six sets of three numbers each add up to 18.

```
                12          11          1

      10                                              4


       8                  17                          3


       9                                              2

                 6           7           5
```

New Order:

Make Up Your Own

How many number sentences can you make using combinations of these numbers? You may use the same number more than once.

Try to use all operations (addition, subtraction, multiplication, division).

6 + 9 = 15

9 − 2 = 7

Vegetable Matters

A vegetable garden was found to have an area of 75 square feet. Draw different shapes that the garden could be and still have the same area.

Draw up a plan for planting the garden so that there are five different vegetables in it, but none take up the same amount of space.

Ten-Pin Puzzle

Each pin below has a point value, shown at the right.

If a black circle shows a knocked down pin, how many points does each pattern show?

What's the highest score possible? _____

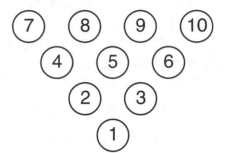

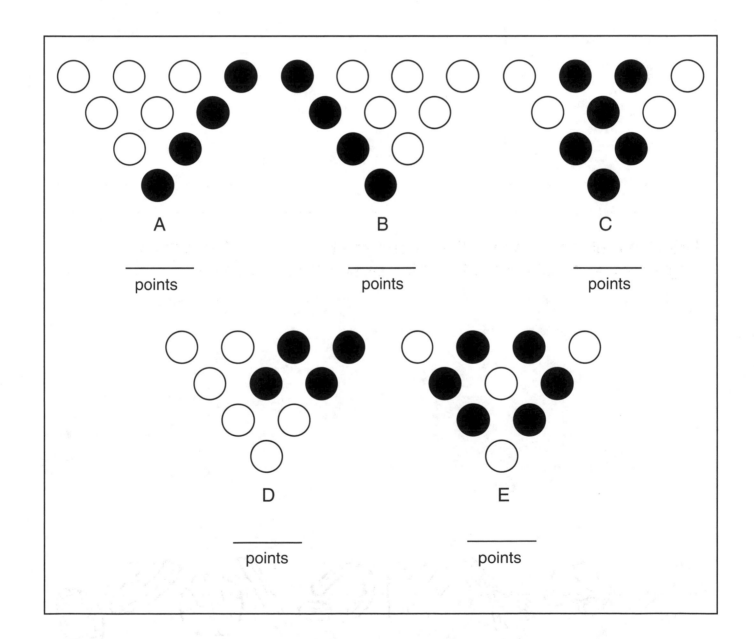

A

_____
points

B

_____
points

C

_____
points

D

_____
points

E

_____
points

Sports Teams

You are to organize the sports teams for your grade. There are 130 students in your grade level, and there are five sports to play. You need to have at least 10 teams.

Solve:

How many students should be on each team? _____

How many reserves do you need for each team? _____

What will you do with the students left over? _____

Triangular Tabulations

How many triangles are there? (Hint: don't forget the upside-down ones or the ones made from other triangles.)

There are _____ triangles.

What Is the Question?

Answer: There were only 14 students left on the bus. Write 10 questions that could fit with this answer.

1. _____
   _____

2. _____
   _____

3. _____
   _____

4. _____
   _____

5. _____
   _____

6. _____
   _____

7. _____
   _____

8. _____
   _____

9. _____
   _____

10. _____
    _____

Looking at Solids

1. How many sports or board games can you name that use some of these solids as part of the playing equipment? Some of the boxes are filled in as an example.

Game	Cube	Rectangle	Triangular Prism	Pyramid	Sphere	Cone	Cylinder
Volleyball		net			ball		
Monopoly	Dice	Money					

Looking at Solids (cont.)

2. Devise a team game or a board game in which at least three solid shapes from the previous page are used.

Number System

Devise a number system to compete with the Roman numeral system. What would the symbols look like and what are they called?

Show what these numbers would look like in your new number system.

7	19	58
257	830	2645

Rewrite these questions using your new number system (and answer them)!

7 + 5 =	20 − 11 =
5 x 10 =	84 ÷ 7 =

Estimation

Estimate how many glasses of water would fill a 10-gallon container.

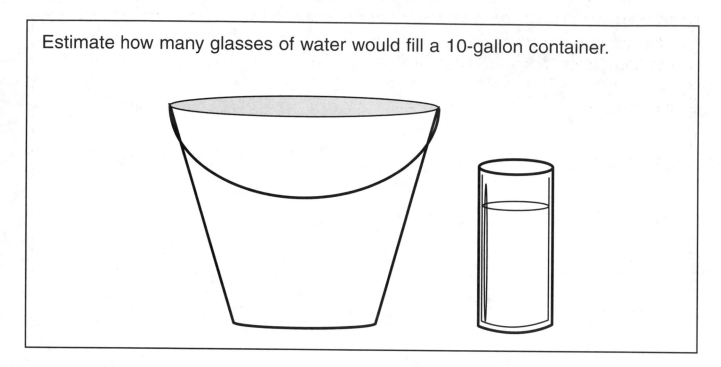

How would you check your answer without pouring the water into the container?

Would this be an accurate way of checking your prediction?

Find the Patterns

The number sentences in each exercise follow a pattern. Find the pattern, continue it for two more lines, and then check your answer on a calculator.

91 x 1 = 91	37 x 3 = 121	9 x 9 + 7 = 88
91 x 2 = 182	37 x 33 = 1221	98 x 9 + 6 = 888
91 x 3 = 273	37 x 333 = 12321	987 x 9 + 5 = 8888

_____   _____   _____

_____   _____   _____

Now make up some number sentences of your own that follow a pattern.

_____   _____   _____

_____   _____   _____

_____   _____   _____

_____   _____   _____

_____   _____   _____

_____   _____   _____

Change the Triangles

Move four toothpicks so that exactly three equilateral triangles are formed.

Strike It Rich!

Whose picture is on the $100,000 bill?

To discover the answer, find the difference in each problem below. Decode the name by matching the answer to its letter. Write the letter in the box below the difference.

9371	3313	4530	6000	6230	3917	6792
− 4528	− 1834	− 3051	− 3781	− 1357	− 2438	− 1949

☐ ☐ ☐ ☐ ☐ ☐ ☐

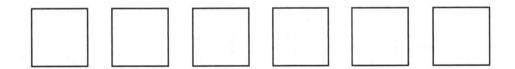

7927	7203	5361	4079	7455	5386
− 3084	− 3427	− 2805	− 2834	− 5976	− 2174

☐ ☐ ☐ ☐ ☐ ☐

1479 **O**	3776 **I**	4843 **W**	2219 **D**
4873 **R**	2556 **L**	3212 **N**	1245 **S**

Did you know?

The $100,000 bill is the highest-value bill ever printed by the United States. It was used only by government banks. The bill is no longer issued.

Birthday Parties

Eight children in one neighborhood will turn 10 this year. From the clues below, determine the month of each child's birthday. Mark the correct boxes with an **X**.

	January 1	February 21	March 25	April 7	May 7	July 15	August 3	October 30
Victor								
Mary								
Marco								
Christina								
Vicky								
Mike								
Danielle								
Peter								

1. Everyone celebrates on Mary's birthday.

2. Danielle's birthday is before Mike's but after Marco's and Victor's.

3. Victor's birthday is exactly one month after Marco's.

4. Christina's birthday is during a winter month.

5. Vicky's birthday comes after Danielle's but before Mike's.

Money Maze

Find your way through the money maze. Mark the path of correct money amounts. You may go $\updownarrow$ $\leftrightarrow$ $\nearrow$ or $\searrow$.

$ End	7 pennies + 7 dimes = 70 cents	**Start $**	4 nickels + 3 dimes = 60 cents
3 pennies + 2 dimes + 2 quarters = 73 cents	4 nickels + 2 dimes + 3 quarters = $1.25	5 nickels + 1 dime + 1 quarter = 55 cents	6 pennies + 6 dimes + 1 quarter = 91 cents
8 pennies + 5 dimes = 58 cents	2 pennies + 3 quarters = 76 cents	8 nickels + 3 quarters = $1.15	11 pennies + 7 dimes = 78 cents
4 quarters + 2 dimes = $1.25	2 pennies + 6 nickels + 7 dimes = $1.02	1 penny + 1 dime + 2 quarters = 61 cents	2 nickels + 3 dimes = 45 cents
8 dimes = 40 cents	17 nickels = 85 cents	7 pennies + 5 nickels = 33 cents	10 quarters = $2.50
2 pennies + 5 nickels + 3 quarters = 87 cents	11 pennies + 4 nickels = 41 cents	7 nickels + 7 dimes = $1.05	3 nickels + 1 dime + 1 quarter = 45 cents
3 pennies + 3 dimes = 35 cents	4 pennies + 7 nickels = 39 cents	3 nickels + 3 dimes + 3 quarters = $1.20	4 pennies + 3 nickels = 19 cents

Solve These If You Can!

Can you find the answers to these word problems?

1. Paul went horseback riding. He paid two five-dollar bills and three quarters. He received one dollar bill and a dime in change. How much did it cost Paul to go riding?

   _____

   _____

2. Amy gave the fast food clerk three one-dollar bills, a quarter, two dimes, and three pennies. The clerk told her she still owes a nickel. How much was Amy's lunch?

   _____

   _____

3. When Lan went bowling, he gave the clerk two one-dollar bills, a half dollar and a quarter. The clerk gave him two dimes in change. How much did it cost Lan to bowl?

   _____

   _____

4. Kimi wanted to buy a cake mix. She looked in her wallet and counted two one-dollar bills and three nickels. She would need a half-dollar more. How much was the cake mix?

   _____

   _____

5. Alvaro bought a ticket to a concert. He paid with a ten-dollar bill and a five-dollar bill. He received two one-dollar bills in change. How much was the concert ticket?

   _____

   _____

6. Sheila wanted to buy a new swimsuit. She had two ten-dollar bills, but would need a five-dollar bill and two one-dollar bills. How much would the new swimsuit cost?

   _____

   _____

What Is on the Road?

Next to each letter of the alphabet, write at least one thing that starts with that letter that you might find beside or on the road. For example: A – ant, ambulance, artwork, arch.

A _____   N _____

B _____   O _____

C _____   P _____

D _____   Q _____

E _____   R _____

F _____   S _____

G _____   T _____

H _____   U _____

I _____   V _____

J _____   W _____

K _____   X _____

L _____   Y _____

M _____   Z _____

What's in the Bag? #1

Read the words on the next page. Then match the letters with the correct synonyms in the clues. (You will not use all of the letters.) Put the five clues together and discover what's in the bag!

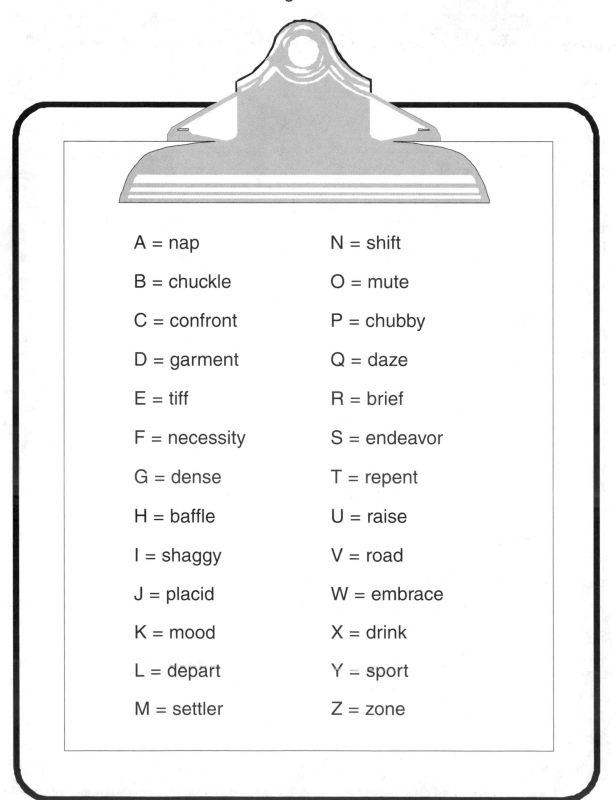

A = nap   N = shift

B = chuckle   O = mute

C = confront   P = chubby

D = garment   Q = daze

E = tiff   R = brief

F = necessity   S = endeavor

G = dense   T = repent

H = baffle   U = raise

I = shaggy   V = road

J = placid   W = embrace

K = mood   X = drink

L = depart   Y = sport

M = settler   Z = zone

What's in the Bag? #1 (cont.)

Clue 1:

———— ———— ———— ————
hug   doze   short   pioneer

Clue 2:

———— ———— ———— ———— ———— ————
region   hairy   plump   plump   dispute   short

Clue 3:

———— ———— ———— ———— ———— ————
plump   doze   clothing   clothing   dispute   clothing

Clue 4:

———— ———— ———— ————
face   doze   pioneer   plump

Clue 5:

———— ———— ————
giggle   dispute   clothing

What's in the bag? _____

What's in the Bag? #2

Read the words on the next page. Then match the letters with the correct synonyms in the clues. (You will not use all of the letters.) Put the five clues together and discover what's in the bag!

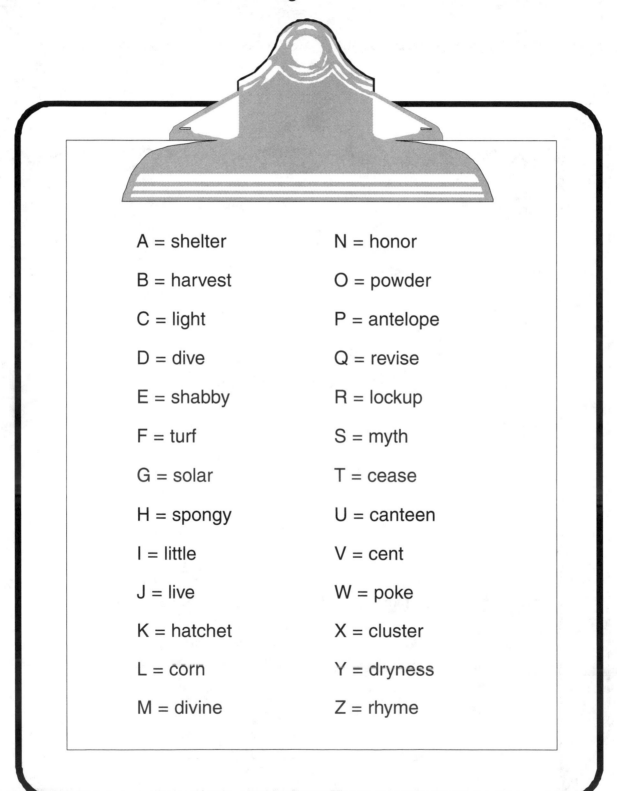

A = shelter

B = harvest

C = light

D = dive

E = shabby

F = turf

G = solar

H = spongy

I = little

J = live

K = hatchet

L = corn

M = divine

N = honor

O = powder

P = antelope

Q = revise

R = lockup

S = myth

T = cease

U = canteen

V = cent

W = poke

X = cluster

Y = dryness

Z = rhyme

What's in the Bag? #2 *(cont.)*

Clue 1:

_____   _____   _____   _____   _____   _____   _____   _____   _____

jail   worn   beam   stop   haven   tribute   sun   maize   worn

Clue 2:

_____   _____   _____   _____   _____   _____

sod   haven   crop   jail   mini   beam

Clue 3:

_____   _____   _____   _____

jab   haven   penny   worn

Clue 4:

_____   _____   _____   _____   _____   _____

fable   drought   godly   crop   dust   maize

Clue 5:

_____   _____   _____   _____   _____   _____

tribute   haven   stop   mini   dust   tribute

What's in the bag? _____

What's in the Bag? #3

Read the words on the next page. Then match the letters with the correct synonyms in the clues. (You will not use all of the letters.) Put the five clues together and discover what's in the bag!

A = abandon   N = needy

B = barbarous   O = option

C = captivity   P = prickly

D = debris   Q = quake

E = exhale   R = recycle

F = flicker   S = ship

G = germinate   T = thread

H = hectic   U = unity

I = immoral   V = violin

J = juvenile   W = wharf

K = kinsman   X = swoop

L = lease   Y = yonder

M = shack   Z = zest

What's in the Bag? #3 *(cont.)*

Clue 1:

_____ _____

choice　　poor

Clue 2:

_____ _____ _____

choice　　sparkle　　sparkle

Clue 3:

_____ _____ _____ _____ _____ _____ _____ _____

thorny　　choice　　reuse　　string　　vacate　　savage　　rent　　breathe

Clue 4:

_____ _____ _____ _____ _____ _____ _____ _____ _____

savage　　vacate　　string　　string　　breathe　　reuse　　evil　　breathe　　yacht

Clue 5:

_____ _____ _____ _____

savage　　breathe　　vacate　　shelter

What's in the bag? _____

What's in the Bag? #4

Read the words on the next page. Then match the letters with the correct synonyms in the clues. (You will not use all of the letters.) Put the five clues together and discover what's in the bag!

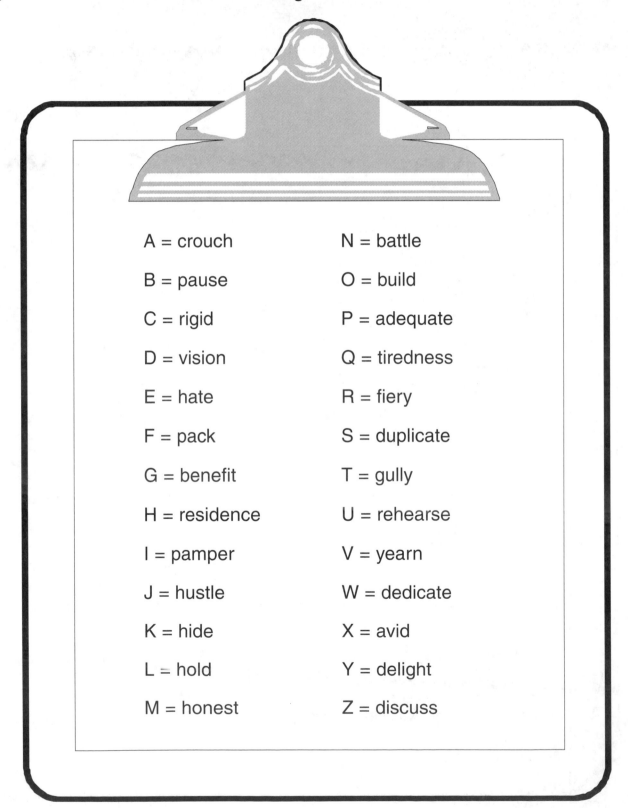

A = crouch	N = battle
B = pause	O = build
C = rigid	P = adequate
D = vision	Q = tiredness
E = hate	R = fiery
F = pack	S = duplicate
G = benefit	T = gully
H = residence	U = rehearse
I = pamper	V = yearn
J = hustle	W = dedicate
K = hide	X = avid
L = hold	Y = delight
M = honest	Z = discuss

128

What's in the Bag? #4 *(cont.)*

Clue 1:

_____ _____ _____ _____ _____ _____
frank   stoop   frank   frank   stoop   retain

Clue 2:

_____ _____ _____ _____ _____ _____
stoop   hot   stiff   ditch   spoil   stiff

Clue 3:

_____ _____ _____ _____ _____ _____ _____
copy   devote   spoil   frank   frank   abhor   hot

Clue 4:

_____ _____ _____ _____ _____ _____ _____
stop   retain   practice stop   stop   abhor   hot

Clue 5:

_____ _____ _____ _____ _____
ditch   practice copy   conceal copy

What's in the bag? _____

Encyclopedias

Encyclopedias have a language all of their own. How many of these encyclopedia-related words can you identify?

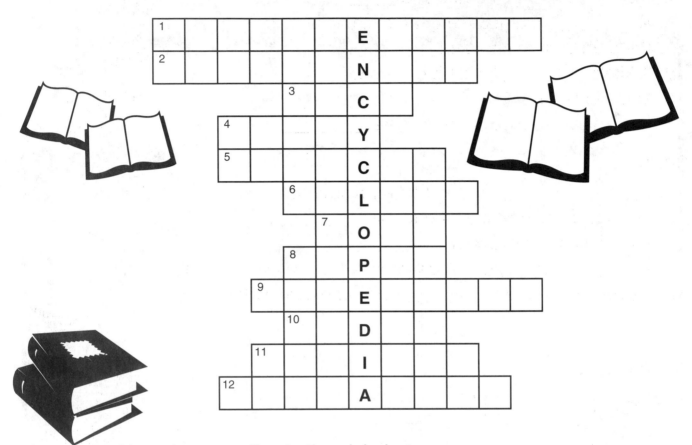

1. arranged in order according to the alphabet

2. a reference book of words and their meanings

3. a piece of true information

4. an item in a reference work

5. a dictionary

6. a book in a set

7. a written or printed work

8. an entry in an encyclopedia

9. a book to which you can refer for facts

10. a list of all main words in a book and their context

11. a section of a reference work

12. a book of synonyms

Kite Safety Rules

Use these clues to solve the puzzle about the important rules of flying kites!

Across

2. Never fly a kite in the rain or a _____.
6. A _____ is a good target for lightning!
7. Keep away from cars and _____.
9. A kite's _____ keeps it balanced.
10. You should follow _____ the safe flying rules.
11. Keep away from buildings and tall _____.

Down

1. _____ _____ will give you a shock if your kite hits them.
3. The kite's string is attached to this: _____.
4. Always fly kites in a wide _____ _____.
5. A _____ is a good place for kite flying.
8. Remember the kite _____ rules and keep safe!

Cheese Words

So many cheeses, so little time to try them all! Can you find them in the puzzle below?

Blue Stilton	Cottage	Munster
Brie	Cream	Parmesan
Camembert	Edam	Ricotta
Cheddar	Mozzarella	Swiss

```
            N   G   I   N   I   C
            O   A   G   A   E   A
P   A   B   T   L   N   S   G   M   M   P   N
R   T   R   L   L   A   E   A   E   U   M   I
A   T   I   I   E   R   M   M   M   N   A   T
D   O   E   T   R   O   R   O   B   S   E   T
D   C   M   S   A   K   A   R   E   T   R   O
E   I   A   E   Z   I   P   F   R   E   C   R
H   R   D   U   Z   K   S   L   T   R   A   C
C   N   E   L   O   E   G   A   T   T   O   C
            B   M   D   B   L   U
            S   S   I   W   S   E
```

Hidden Words

How many words of four or more letters beginning with **S** can you make from the word saxophone?

_____   _____

_____   _____

_____   _____

_____   _____

_____   _____

_____   _____

The Mercedes Wheel

Here's a Mercedes wheel. How many words can you make by traveling from one letter to the next along the lines? You can't use a letter twice unless it's on the wheel twice.

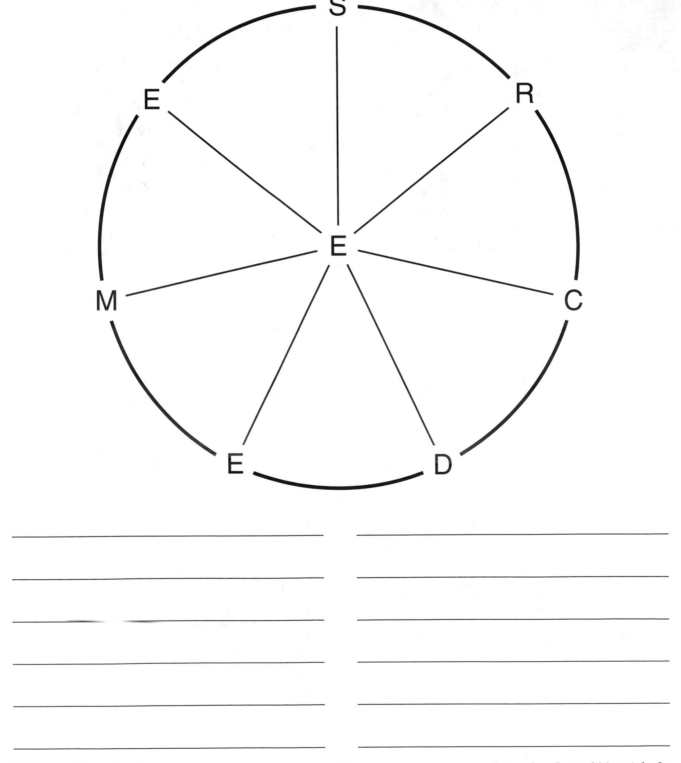

Solar System Mystery

Here are the nine planets of the solar system. Look very carefully at their spelling. Can you give three reasons why Mars's name is the odd one out?

Mars's name is the odd one out because:

1. _____

   _____

2. _____

   _____

3. _____

   _____

Something Old, Something New

Traditionally, a bride wears something old and something new. Can you turn old into new in nine tries by changing one letter at a time? Only use the clues if you really have to!

O	L	D	
			not even
			increase by several
			help
			a cover
			caused to burn
			a small bug egg
			opposite of "is"
			a fish trap
N	E	W	

Inside the Hindenberg

How many words of four or more letters can you make from the word Hindenberg?

HINDENBERG

Four-letter words:

Five-letter words:

Six-letter words:

Seven-letter words:

Eight-letter words:

Spot the Sea Monster!

If you are going to survive on the seven seas, you'll need to be able to identify and name these creatures (mythical and real) of the deep. You may need to do some research to solve this puzzle.

1. common fast-moving ten-armed mollusk
2. the largest mythical monster
3. a carnivorous marine fish with tough skin
4. a burrowing marine mollusk
5. home of the mythical Scottish sea serpent
6. large venomous ray with barbed spines
7. a snake-like sea creature
8. eight-legged sea creature
9. huge marine mammal
10. mythical Norwegian sea-monster

End with a Nap

Can you make a bed? Into a cot? Then end with a nap? Just change one letter at a time to make the next word. Use the clues to help.

B	E	D	
			a wager
			a striking implement
			feline
C	O	T	
			policeman
			type of hat
N	A	P	

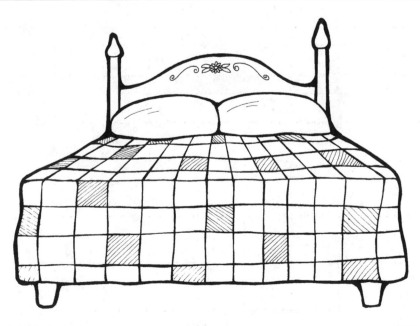

Bikinis!

Bikini has an unusual pattern of letters:
consonant-vowel-consonant-vowel-consonant-vowel.

Even more uncommon is the reverse pattern:
vowel-consonant-vowel-consonant-vowel-consonant.

Here are some words based on those patterns. Can you identify them all?

	a		a		a	Mexican musical instrument
	a		a		a	large desert
	a		a		a	tropical fruit
	a		a		a	a type of hat; a canal
	e		e		e	erase
	e		e		e	calm
	o		o		o	part of a pirate chant
e		e		e		a number
e		e		e		a metal ring for lining a small hole

Library Find-a-Word

Find the words below. The unused letters will spell out a place where family or institutional records are kept.

author, book, catalogue, Dewey, dictionary, due, file, index, lend, librarian, library, overdue, Q (found on the spine of the Quarto books), reference, shelf, stacks, tome, volume.

```
F  E  L  I  F  D  E  W  E  Y
L  M  S  K  C  A  T  S  R  R
E  U  G  O  L  A  T  A  C  A
H  L  D  U  E  O  N  A  R  R
S  O  C  H  M  O  K  O  O  B
I  V  V  E  I  X  E  D  N  I
L  A  U  T  H  O  R  Q  E  L
E  E  C  N  E  R  E  F  E  R
N  I  S  O  V  E  R  D  U  E
D  L  I  B  R  A  R  I  A  N
```

Family or institutional records are kept in _____.

It's Not That Easy Being Green

Each of the words or phrases starts with green. Work them all out and your friends will be green with envy!

Clue	
greenish pest on garden plants	
a long thin vegetable	
a large cold island to the north	
American slang for paper money	
a building with glass walls	
a signal to proceed	
a special ability to make plants grow	
a vegetable that is hollow inside	
a merchant who sells fresh foodstuffs	
someone in charge of lawns and grounds	

Partial answers filled in: F L Y / B E A N

G R E E N

International Police

Police forces exist in almost every country of the world, and it's handy to know who to ask for when you're traveling. So here are the names of six police forces. Take away the extra letters and unjumble them to find out what nationality the force is. Get on the beat!

polizel: manger = _____

politie: touched – oe = _____

polizia: mail train – mr = _____

policia: happiness – ep = _____

gendarme: arch-felon – alo = _____

mounties: ball and chain – bhll = _____

Coats

What kind of coat goes on best when it's wet—and stays on best when its dry? Find each of these coats in the word search grid. Then rearrange the missing letters.

anorak	jacket	sport coat
blazer	mackintosh	topcoat
bolero	overcoat	tuxedo
bomber	parka	windbreaker
fur	ski	wrap

```
A  R  U  F  C              O  P  A  T  S
S  P  O  R  T  C  O  A  T  O  F  A  P  K
A  R  E  K  A  E  R  B  D  N  I  W  R  I
H  S  O  T  N  I  K  C  A  M  O  I  N  W
      T  T  T  A  B  O  R  V
      U  A  E  N  L  R  E  E
      X  O  K  O  A  E  B  R
      E  C  C  R  Z  L  M  C
      D  P  A  A  E  O  O  O
      O  O  J  K  R  B  B  A
      T  T  P  A  R  K  A  T
```

Answer: _____

More Proverbial Codes

Use the code in the box to crack the code below and finish the sentences.

Letter	m	n	o	p	q	r	s	t	u	v	w	x	y
Code	A	B	C	D	E	F	G	H	I	J	K	L	M

Letter	z	a	b	c	d	e	f	g	h	i	j	k	l
Code	N	O	P	Q	R	S	T	U	V	W	X	Y	Z

1. Don't (oagzf) _____ your (otuowqze) _____ before
   they (tmfot) _____.

2. Birds of a (rqmftqd) _____ flock (fasqftqd) _____.

3. A (efufot) _____ in (fuyq) _____ saves
   (zuzq) _____.

4. A (bqzzk) _____ saved is a (bqzzk)_____
   (qmdzqp) _____.

5. Two (idazse)_____ don't make a (dustf) _____.

6. Where there is a (iuxx) _____, there is a (imk) _____.

7. (efduwq) _____ while the (udaz) _____ is hot.

8. A (imfotqp) _____ pot never (nauxe) _____.

Frontier Words

Frontier living generated many new words that were commonly used by the pioneers. Figure out these words by reading the clues first. Then find the coordinates on the grid below.

Write the letter that is in that space on the proper lines. (To find the coordinates, go across the first number of spaces. From there, count up the second number of spaces.)

4	l	d	s	i	g	e	m	c	p	s	u	g	l	a	t
3	f	e	a	n	r	o	i	u	i	h	e	u	o	n	d
2	p	o	h	e	m	a	s	f	c	y	m	t	p	r	s
1	c	a	e	y	l	t	g	r	o	n	d	o	a	f	s
0	1	2	3	4	5	6	7	8	9	10	11	12	13	14	15

1. ___ ___ ___ ___ ___ is a prairie sod house.
   3,4 13,3 2,4 11,1 10,2

2. ___ ___ ___ ___   ___ ___ ___ ___ ___ ___ ___ are also known as johnnycakes.
   8,4 9,1 5,3 4,3   15,3 2,2 2,4 5,4 6,4 14,2 7,2

3. ___ ___ ___ ___ ___ - ___ ___ ___ ___ ___ ___ rushed to California to find gold.
   8,2 12,1 8,1 15,4 4,1   4,3 7,3 10,1 3,1 5,3 10,4

4. ___ ___ ___ ___ ___ are dried buffalo manure used for fires.
   8,4 3,2 9,3 13,2 3,4

5. ___ ___ ___ ___ ___ ___ ___ ___ ___ are settlers of the western frontier.
   4,2 7,4 4,4 7,1 5,3 2,1 14,3 6,1 7,2

6. ___ ___ ___ ___ is a disease now known as malaria.
   6,2 12,4 8,3 11,3

7. ___ ___ ___ ___ ___ ___ ___ ___ are thieves who stole cattle.
   5,3 11,4 15,2 6,1 13,4 2,3 8,1 15,1

8. prairie ___ ___ ___ ___ ___ ___ ___ ___ is a nickname for a covered wagon.
   7,2 1,1 10,3 2,2 9,1 14,3 3,1 5,3

Palindromes

Palindromes are words, phrases, sentences, or numbers that read the same forward and backward. Write a palindrome that relates to each word or phrase below. An example has been done for you.

12 o'clock = noon

1. distress call _____

2. organ to see with _____

3. quiet _____

4. by yourselves _____

5. dad _____

6. amazing _____

7. little child _____

8. radio tracker _____

9. a joke _____

10. female parent _____

11. short for Robert _____

12. woman's name _____

13. term of respect for a woman _____

14. The paper that says you own property _____

15. female sheep _____

Meteorite Mix-Up

It's amazing what you can find hidden inside a meteorite. What can you find in the letters of the word "meteorite"? The black squares are the letters not used in the answer. Unscramble the remaining ones for the answer.

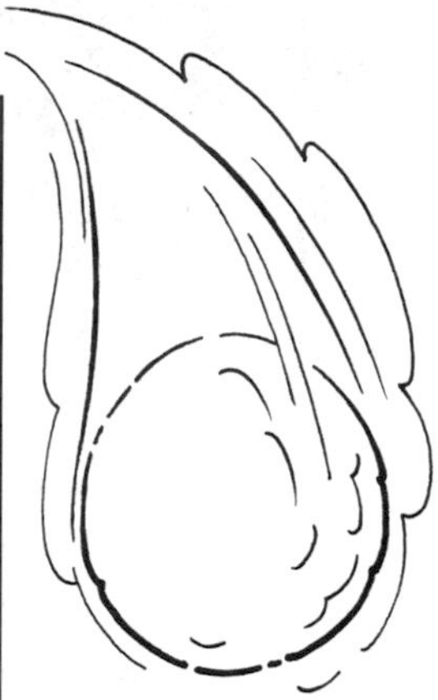

	M	E	T	E	O	R	I	T	E
Woody plant with trunk and branches	■			■	■		■	■	
To remove the edges		■		■	■			■	■
Mysterious	■		■		■			■	
Deserve		■	■		■				■
100 cm		■	■		■		■		
Aquatic mammal with gnawing teeth	■	■					■		■
Clock that measures a time interval		■			■			■	■
A section of a school year			■	■	■		■		■
Far away							■	■	■
Whitish insect that feeds on wood					■				■

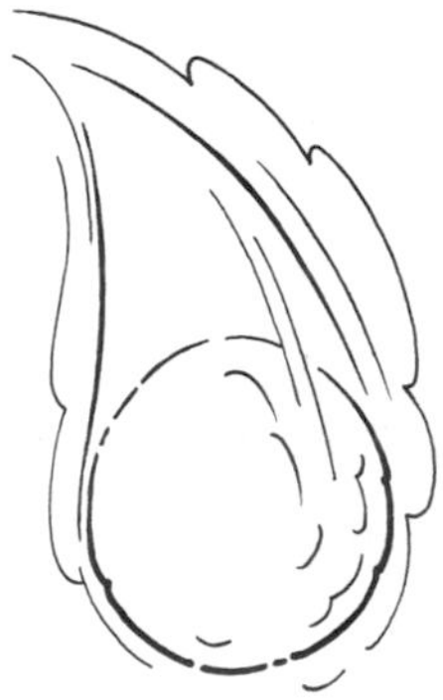

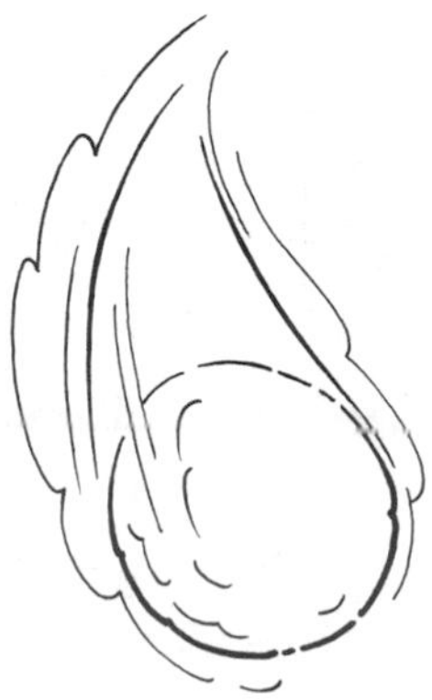

Publishing Sports

Write a plan to show how you would make a book on a sport. Include the following in your plan:

- where you would get photos, etc.
- whom you would interview for first hand knowledge about the sport
- the style of the book

Safari

Imagine you have been given the task of organizing an African safari. Plan your advertising campaign to attract people to join you.

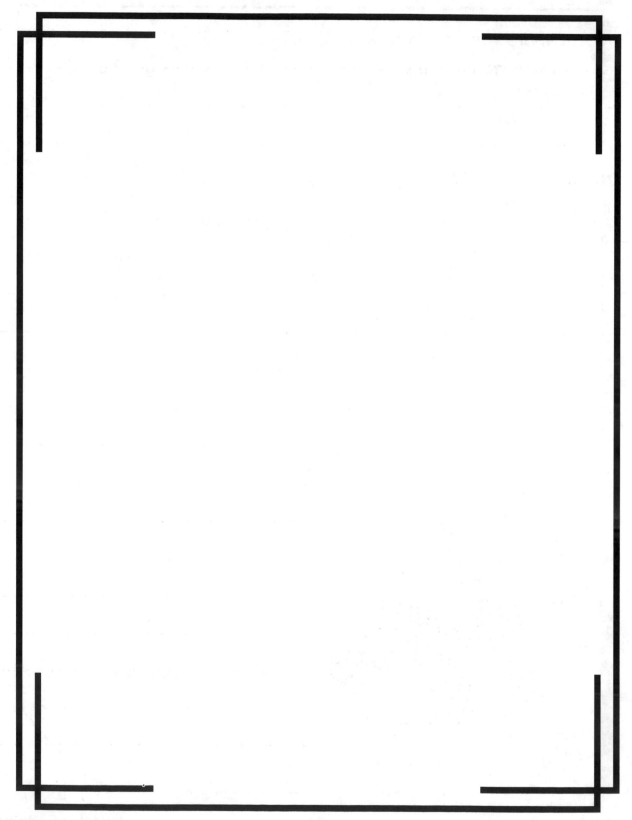

My Favorite Animal

If you could choose to be one animal that lives in the African jungle, which animal would you choose, and why?

_____

_____

_____

_____

_____

_____

_____

_____

_____

_____

_____

_____

_____

_____

_____

_____

_____

_____

_____

Fairy Tales

What might the cow have seen when she jumped over the moon? _____

_____

_____

_____

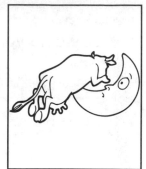

Brainstorm all the possible ways that Little Bo Peep could locate her sheep. _____

_____

_____

_____

What are 10 other unusual names instead of Rumpelstiltskin? _____

_____

_____

_____

_____

_____

_____

_____

_____

_____

_____

What are some of the dreams that Sleeping Beauty could have had? _____

_____

_____

Brainstorm questions you would like to ask the Magic Mirror. _____

_____

_____

Funny Conversations

Make up a play about a conversation between:

Pinnochio and Humpty Dumpty
or
The Ugly Duckling and Snow White's Stepmother
or
Baby Bear and the Pied Piper

Letter of Complaint

Write a letter from Papa Bear to Goldilocks' mother complaining of her daughter's behavior, and in the letter list the damage she has caused.

_____,

_____

_____

_____

_____

_____

_____

_____

_____

_____

                                    _____,

                                    _____

Redesign Your Classroom

Improve your classroom so that it becomes more unusual and an exciting place to be. Begin by listing what you do not like about the room and then think creatively about the changes that you can make.

Things I do not like:

_____

_____

_____

_____

_____

_____

Changes I would make:

_____

_____

_____

_____

_____

_____

Communicating in Code

Different kinds of languages and codes have also been created to help people who can't see or hear well to communicate. Here is what the Braille alphabet would look like if it were printed in black and white instead of raised dots on a page which a blind person would read by touch.

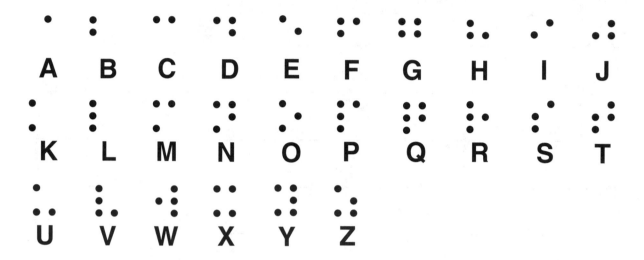

If you couldn't speak or hear, you would still be able to read, but how would you talk to your friends or family? One way would be to use your hands. Here is the Sign Language Manual Alphabet.

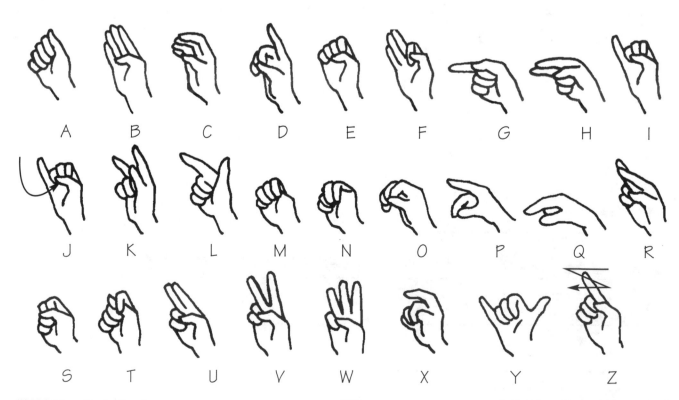

Communicating in Code *(cont.)*

Make a code that you could use to write a paragraph about yourself. Use the space below to create your code. The symbols you use can be art or geometric forms, numbers, letters, dots and dashes, or any combination. Include things like where you were born, how many brothers or sisters you have, your favorite subject, food, sport, etc. Write the paragraph on the lines below.

My Code

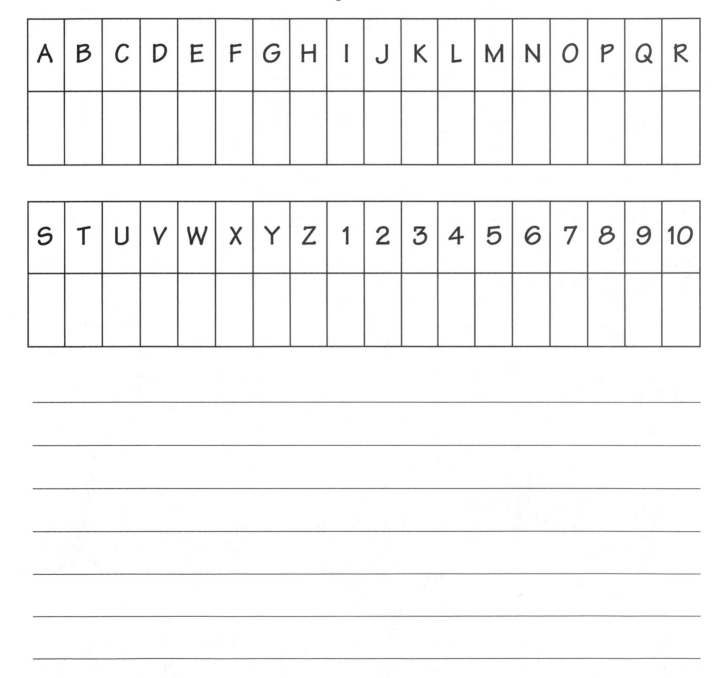

A	B	C	D	E	F	G	H	I	J	K	L	M	N	O	P	Q	R

S	T	U	V	W	X	Y	Z	1	2	3	4	5	6	7	8	9	10

_____

_____

_____

_____

_____

_____

Your Senses

How do your senses help you to learn?

Write about each one:

sight _____

hearing _____

smell _____

taste _____

touch _____

Which sense do you think we depend upon most? Why?

_____

_____

_____

_____

More Senses

Why do some people love the taste of a particular food, while other people don't like it at all?

_____

_____

_____

_____

Why does a bump on the nose hurt more than a similar bump on your arm or leg?

_____

_____

_____

_____

Why does a minute particle of grit cause real pain when it is in your eye, but doesn't bother you if it is in your hair?

_____

_____

_____

_____

A New Game

Prepare a storyboard to advertise the new basketball game you have invented. Use the boxes to draw your cartoons, and put any dialogue, directions, special effects, or music in the lines below. These boxes will be used to develop the script for the promotional commercial of your new game.

I have called my new version of basketball:_____.

1.

2.

3.

_____

4.

5.

6.

Clean Up!

Create a "clean up the garden" machine. Draw it and explain how it works.

How it works:

_____

_____

_____

_____

_____

_____

_____

_____

_____

Dinosaur Expedition

You are heading an expedition to capture the last living dinosaur in a remote part of the world.

1. Describe it and explain how it managed to survive.

_____

_____

_____

_____

2. Devise a plan to capture it.

_____

_____

_____

3. How would you look after it until experts arrived?

_____

_____

_____

_____

Extinction

The answer is "extinction."

Write ten questions for this answer.

1. _____

2. _____

3. _____

4. _____

5. _____

6. _____

7. _____

8. _____

9. _____

10. _____

A Brand New Pastime

Imagine that you are not able to do any of your favorite activities (no television, computer, CD's, radio, games, or books) for a whole week! Devise a new hobby to occupy your time.

_____

_____

_____

_____

_____

_____

_____

_____

_____

_____

_____

_____

Popular Hobbies

Can you name five hobbies that would be suitable for older people? _____

_____   _____   _____   _____

Why do you think they would be suitable?

_____

_____

_____

_____

Can you name five hobbies that would be suitable for children aged 10 and under?

_____

_____

_____

_____

Why do you think they would be suitable?

_____

_____

_____

_____

Patterns

Design the school's new sports uniform.

You may only use two colors and you must include three connecting shapes. The pattern is to be repeated over the whole uniform.

The colors I have chosen are _____ and _____.

Draw the three shapes you will use here.

My pattern will look like this:

Now choose a new pattern of your own.

I have decided to use _____ colors.

These will be: _____

I have decided to use _____ connecting shapes.

These will be:

My pattern will look like this:

Communication Types

Fill in the table below. In column two, check if you use the communication methods listed. In columns three and four, write down who would or would not use the communication methods listed. Give as many answers as you can.

1. Method	2. You	3. Would use	4. Would not use
Speech			
Letters			
Telephone			
Radio			
Television			
Art			
Music			
Books/Stories			
Computer			
Drums			
Smoke			
Dance			
Telegraph			

Imagine

1. Imagine you were to step back in time. Explain how you would have communicated with other people.

---

2. Now imagine you step forward in time. Explain what you think your relatives will be using to communicate with people in another city 100 years from now. Write a description and draw a picture below.

Signs and Logos

What are some of the most common signs and logos that you see every day in your community? Illustrate your favorite ones. (Remember that correct color is often the most important part of the plan.)

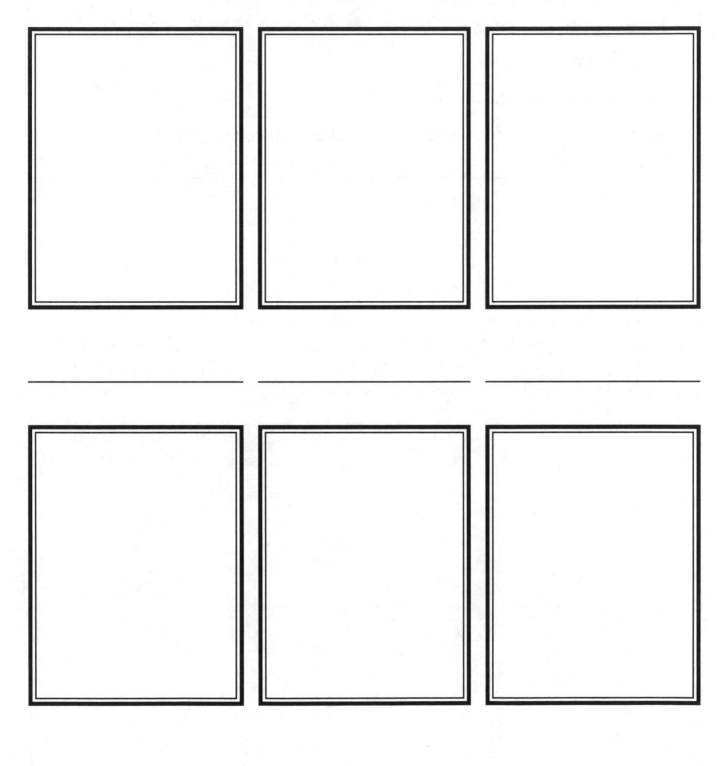

Game Plan

Invent a new game that requires players to . . .

- run, hop, and jump

- touch, catch, and throw

- twist, stretch, and bend

- use one piece of equipment.

The area of play must not be larger than half a basketball court.

Math Mystery

Fred's father is a lawyer who carries a briefcase. On the morning of Fred's birthday, Fred's father left his briefcase at home. While Fred was getting ready for school, he found a note his father left him about solving the math mystery. It was related to the birthday present left inside the briefcase. Fred must solve the math mystery to unlock his father's briefcase to get his birthday present. Here are the clues that Fred's father left behind.

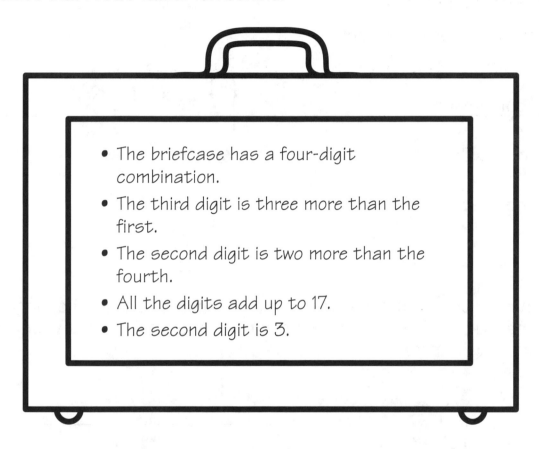

- The briefcase has a four-digit combination.
- The third digit is three more than the first.
- The second digit is two more than the fourth.
- All the digits add up to 17.
- The second digit is 3.

Here's a hint that you might find useful to solve the mystery.

- Use algebraic equations and assign each digit with a different unknown variable. For example, the first digit of the four-digit combination could be *a*, the second digit could be *b*, etc. By applying this hint, you already know that $b = 3$ because this information is given to you.

Use the clues above along with this hint to solve the math mystery.

What is the four-digit combination for the briefcase?

Dance Diagrams

You might not find people waltzing in a disco, but the waltz is certainly danced in many other places! Read the instructions while you follow the diagram.

1. left foot forward

2. right foot to side

3. left foot up to right foot

4. right foot forward

5. left foot to side

6. right foot up to left foot

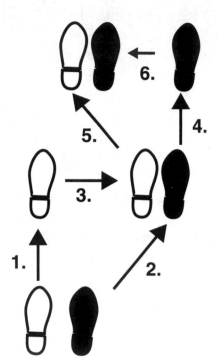

Now you are an expert on the waltz! Write the instructions for the tango by following the diagram. Use the dance diagrams and try the steps yourself. For fun, invent a new dance!

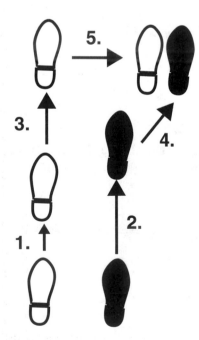

1. _____

2. _____

3. _____

4. _____

5. _____

Investigative Journalist

Kelly Sly has given this story to her editor, who finds new mistakes—seven to be precise! Can you find them all?

I visited the harbor on Saturday, September 31. I was after a gang of smugglers operating out of a four-engine sailboat docked at pier 3. A quick view of the vessel showed the anchor safely pulled up. I walked up the gangplank onto the deck and looked for somewhere to hide. A barrel full of ropes seemed ideal, so I climbed in and waited. It wasn't long before some men appeared. "We share the loot three ways, like we always do," said one. The others nodded sullenly. Unfortunately, I chose that moment to sneeze. They were onto me immediately, dragging me from the tight funnel. "A spy! Throw her overboard!" cried the one with the black long-sleeved shirt and the tattoos on his back. "Look behind you!" I screamed, and as they turned, I dove into the murky river. Unfortunately, the smugglers spotted me and finished me with a fatal shot.

1. _____

2. _____

3. _____

4. _____

5. _____

6 _____

7. _____

On the Farm

Farmer Kelly has very kindly donated 1/4 of his land to the local school for a new playground. He's also given the school a long roll of barbed wire and some rules.

1. Each of his three prize cows must have her own separate paddock.

2. The three paddocks and the playground must be exactly the same size and shape.

3. Each of the cows must be able to lean over her fence and look into the playground.

How did the school do it?

_____

_____

_____

_____

Solar System Mnemonics

It is difficult to explore the frontiers of space if you don't even know the planets of your own solar system. There are nine of them and its easy to mix them up, so what you need is a mnemonic. A mnemonic is a memory aid.

For example, Many Various Elephants Munch Jam So Underwater Numbats Purr. Confused? Each initial letter represents the initial letter of a planet. So: Many = Mercury, Various = Venus, and so on.

If you don't think much of munching elephants, make up your own! Here are the planets (in order):

Mercury, Venus, Earth, Mars, Jupiter, Saturn, Uranus, Neptune, Pluto.

The sillier the better, so go for it!

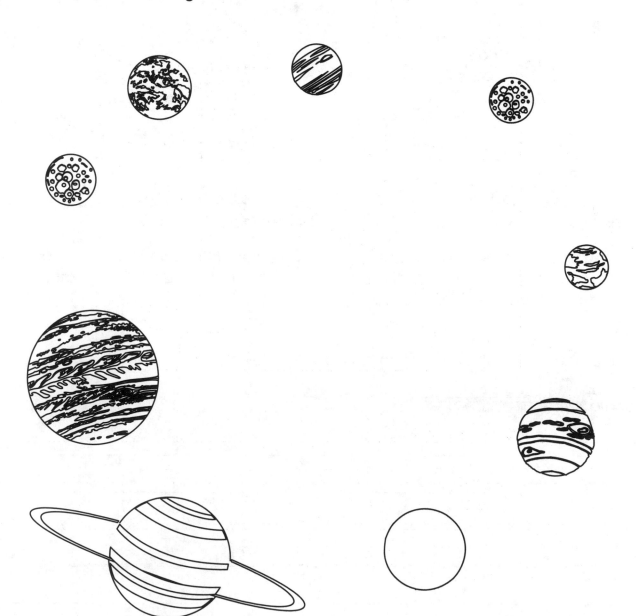

Questions and Answers

Match the question with the answer.

1. _____   2. _____   3. _____   4. _____

1. What would happen if you won the lottery?

2. Which is better, a chocolate ice cream or a caramel sundae?

3. Which day of the week do you like best?

4. How would you make a cake?

Answers:

A. A sundae is better because you can have nuts on top.

B. Turn on the oven, then put all the ingredients in a bowl, mix them, and put them in the oven to cook.

C. Sunday is best because I go out with Mom and Dad.

D. I would be able to buy lots of different things for my family.

Choose one of the above questions and write down five different answers.

Question: _____

Answers:

1. _____

2. _____

3. _____

4. _____

5. _____

Fairy Tale Questions

What if a fairy godmother had a chance to restock Old Mother Hubbard's shelves? What would she put inside?

How could you redesign the house of the old woman who lived in a shoe, so that she and her children could live underwater?

Helicopters

1. Draw a helicopter and label it.   Draw an airplane and label it.

2. List ways in which helicopters and planes are used to help people.

Helicopters	**Planes**
_____	_____
_____	_____
_____	_____
_____	_____

3. Describe how helicopters take off. What is the main difference between helicopters and planes in their take-off procedures?

4. Which aircraft would be more suitable in these situations?
   Explain why you think so.

• Transporting workers to an off-shore oil rig	• Taking a concert group to another state to perform
• Herding cattle in the outback	• Taking people in a parachuting contest to the drop off point

Hobbies That Earn Money

How many hobbies can you think of that could earn money?

The Environment

Record the changes in our environment by studying each of the listed areas. The first one has been done for you as an example.

Place	Description	Habitat For	Threatened By	If Lost	Can Be Protected By
Beach	sand, water, shells	crabs, fish, birds	people leaving their garbage lying around	nowhere to swim or sail	people picking up their own garbage
School Yard					
Park					
Rain Forest					
Wet Lands					

Listing Ideas

List objects that have a handle.

_____

_____

_____

_____

List words that have to do with feeling happy.

_____

_____

_____

_____

List three syllable words (for example ex-cite-ment).

_____

_____

_____

_____

List as many rhyming-word pairs as you can (for example a black sack, a big pig).

_____

_____

_____

_____

What a Ladder!

Example:

 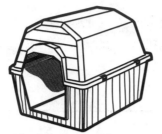  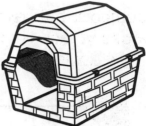

1. Dog kennel.

2. Make it Bigger. This will give the dog more room.

3. Add bedding and windows for greater comfort.

4. Replace the simple wooden walls with brick for better insulation against the cold.

Now you try it!

Redesign the stepladder using the BAR strategy (explained below). Draw and explain each change. 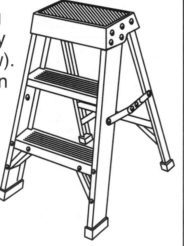	**B** Make it **b**igger Reasons: _____ _____
A **A**dd something Reasons: _____	**R** **R**eplace, change, or rearrange Reasons: _____

A New Body

If you had the imaginative task of redesigning the human body, think about the changes you could make. Draw the changed body and list the advantages of the new design.

Create a New Cage

Help redesign this monkey's cage. Draw and explain each change.

A Time Capsule

Imagine that you have to choose 10 personal items to fit in a time capsule. You have been asked to choose items that would use each of the senses. What would you include? Explain the reasons for each choice.

Choice	Reasons
1. _____	_____
2. _____	_____
3. _____	_____
4. _____	_____
5. _____	_____
6. _____	_____
7. _____	_____
8. _____	_____
9. _____	_____
10. _____	_____

Think carefully about what you could include in a 30-word message to go in your time capsule. What would you like people to know about this time and the way you live?

_____

_____

_____

Finding Attributes

List the attributes of each of the objects below.
An example has been done for you. Choose some
attributes to link together to form a new object.
Describe this new object and draw it below.

playful · purrs · affectionate · warm · **cat** · furry · cuddles · scratches · independent

playful · **child**

daffodil

Description of new object:	Drawing:
_____	
_____	
_____	
_____	
_____	

Make Them Interesting!

Turn these shapes into different, creative, and interesting objects or people.
While drawing, you can turn the page to face any direction.

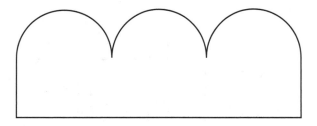

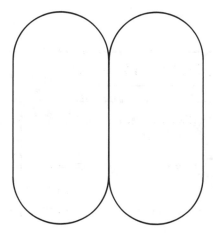

Hidden Meanings

Explain the meaning of each box.

F Ⅎ A ∀ C Ɔ E Ǝ	**man** ——— **board**	LE VEL
1. _____	2. _____	3. _____

wear
———
long
	d
	d e e r
	  e
	  r
		HEAD
		———
		HEELS

4. _____	5. _____	6. _____

businesspleasure	coORDERurt	N W O T
7. _____	8. _____	9. _____

Ban ana	0 ——— B.S. M.A. Ph.D.	sota
10. _____	11. _____	12. _____

Brain Challenges

Scrambled Math

Can you unscramble the following words to find the math terms? Write the correct word on the line after each scrambled word.

1. dad _____

2. mus _____

3. roze _____

4. lahf _____

5. slup _____

6. sinum _____

7. nitodida _____

8. geanevit _____

9. gidit _____

10. citsaamthem _____

11. trasucbt _____

12. simet _____

13. viddie _____

14. tracifon _____

15. bumner _____

How Many?

1. sides in a dodecagon? _____

2. items in a baker's dozen? _____

3. rings on the Olympic flag? _____

4. years in a century? _____

5. original colonies in the United States? _____

6. sides does a pentagon have? _____

7. wheels on a unicycle? _____

8. hours in a week? _____

9. days in a leap year? _____

10. years in a millennium? _____

11. cards in a standard deck? _____

12. centimeters in a meter? _____

13. degrees in a right angle? _____

14. planets in our solar system? _____

15 eyes on a Cyclops? _____

16. keys on a piano? _____

17. bones in a human body? _____

18. degrees in a circle? _____

19. events are in a decathlon? _____

20. squares on a checkerboard? _____

Choices

The following exercises are taken from real-life examples. The answer to each is found in how often you intend to buy or use the product or service. Answer the question by showing your work on each.

A Mexican restaurant sells tacos for $1.50. As part of their special "Taco Thursday" promotion, if you wear a T-shirt printed with the restaurant logo that advertises "Taco Thursday," you can buy the tacos for $1.25 each. The shirt costs $12.99. Should you buy a shirt? Will you really save money on the tacos? What other factors are there?

_____

_____

_____

Your friend's mother has a car and is willing to drive you to school for $25 a month or 10 cents a mile. Suppose you live 2.7 miles from the school. Calculate which deal you should take. Consider your other options.

_____

_____

_____

Writing Numbers

The numbers we use are called Arabic numbers. They were first developed in India and introduced to the rest of the world by Arab traders. This system gained popularity because it was far easier to use than most of the previous number systems. One of the most important concepts that the Arabs helped to introduce was zero. Without zero, our decimal system would not be possible. The following table shows the first 11 numbers in five other systems. Note that the ancient Mayans also discovered and used a symbol for zero.

Arabic	1	2	3	4	5	6	7	8	9	10	11
Babylonian	▼	▼▼	▼▼▼	▼▼▼▼	▼▼▼ ▼▼	▼▼▼ ▼▼▼	▼▼▼▼ ▼▼▼	▼▼▼▼ ▼▼▼▼	▼▼▼ ▼▼▼ ▼▼▼	<	<▼
Egyptian	I	II	III	IIII	II III	III III	III IIII	IIII IIII	IIII IIIII	Ω	Ω I
Roman	I	II	III	IV	V	VI	VII	VIII	IX	X	XI
Mayan	○	○○	○○○	○○○○	____	○	○○	○○○	○○○○	═══	○ ═══
Base 2	1	10	11	100	101	110	111	1000	1001	1010	1011

Use the patterns above to extend each system to show the numbers 12 to 20.

Arabic	12	13	14	15	16	17	18	19	20
Babylonian									
Egyptian									
Roman									
Mayan									
Base 2									

"Sum" Triangle

Arrange the numbers 1–6 with one in each circle so the sum along each side of the triangle is the same. If done correctly, each triangle will have a different answer. Write the answer for each triangle in the center circle. One number for each sum is given. **Hint:** The four sums are consecutive numbers.

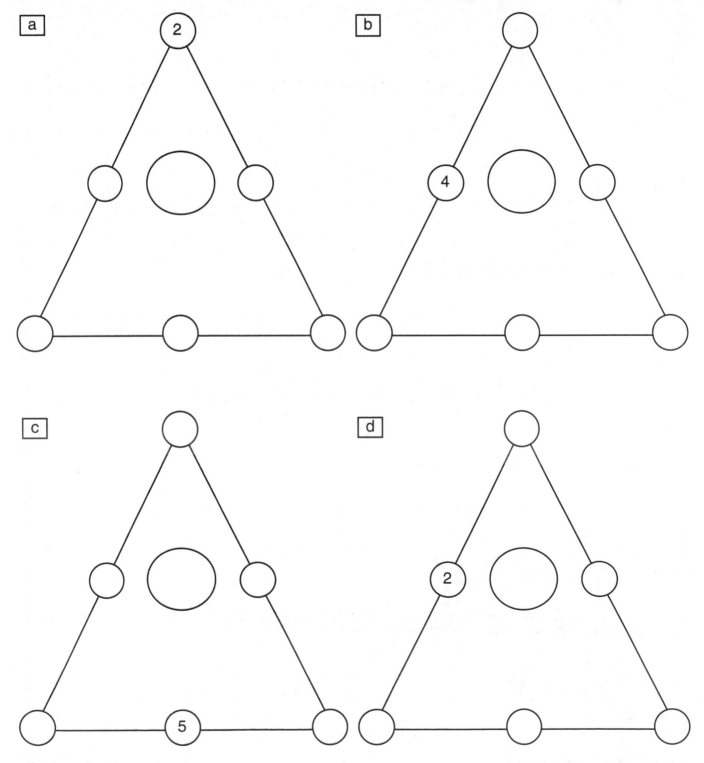

Estimation

1. Estimate how many jelly beans would fit into a one-gallon container.

_____

_____

_____

2. How could you check your answer without actually counting the jelly beans?

_____

_____

_____

3. Would this be a reliable method?

_____

_____

_____

4. Give reasons for your answer.

_____

_____

_____

Math Fair

Your school is going to have a math fair. Design a poster to advertise your presentation stating why it is the best topic to be presented at the fair.

Math Names

What is the correct name for the objects described below?

Description	Name	Description	Name
500 sheets of paper		200th anniversary	
Dinosaur with three horns on its head		Married to two people at the same time	
Four babies at the same time to one mother		Roman officer in charge of 100 soldiers	
Six-pointed star		10-event athletic competition	
Three-sided figure		5-event athletic competition	

Credit Card Capers

Credit cards have a 16 digit number, such as 4567 6002 0762 3535. What's unusual about each of these credit card numbers?

1. 2884 4646 2228 8422

_____

2. 1009 8423 3248 9001

_____

3. 0537 1074 2148 4296

_____

4. 1991 3357 9113 9711

_____

5. 5238 1654 9858 1234

_____

6. 1113 2317 3719 2931

_____

7. 1248 1632 6412 8256

_____

8. 1500 2534 4104 8138

_____

9. 0088 5489 3774 0648

_____

10. 0003 1854 9203 1184 (c = 3, r=18, etc.)

_____

Number Challenge

Use the numbers below to total 100, without rearranging the order. You can add, subtract, multiply or divide.

1 2 3 4 5 6 7 8 9

Can you think of a way to make them total 50?

Consecutive Numbers

Consecutive numbers are those which follow each other in counting order, for example: 2, 3, 4.

Many numbers can be made by adding consecutive numbers, for example:

$9 = 4 + 5$ and $10 = 1 + 2 + 3 + 4$

Beside each number below, show the consecutive numbers which add up to make that original number. (Do not use zero.)

Are there any you can't do?

1 = _____	16 = _____
2 = _____	17 = _____
3 = _____	18 = _____
4 = _____	19 = _____
5 = _____	20 = _____
6 = _____	21 = _____
7 = _____	22 = _____
8 = _____	23 = _____
9 = _____	24 = _____
10 = _____	25 = _____
11 = _____	26 = _____
12 = _____	27 = _____
13 = _____	28 = _____
14 = _____	29 = _____
15 = _____	30 = _____

Decimal and Binary Numbers

Computer don't work with decimal numbers. Instead, they use binary numbers, or "ons" and "offs." The binary numbers **1** is "on" and **0** is "off." In decimal numbers 11,101 =

1 ten-thousand + 1 thousand + 1 hundred + 0 tens + 1 one.

In binary numbers 11101 =

1 sixteen + 1 eight + 1 four + 0 twos + 1 one. This is the number 29 in decimal.

Can you change these binary numbers into decimal numbers?

1. 100 = (1 four + 0 twos + 0 ones) = _____

2. 110 = _____

3. 1001 = _____

4. 10101 = _____

5. 11111 = _____

Now change these decimal numbers into binary numbers:

6. 19 _____

7. 7 _____

8. 25 _____

9. 10 _____

10. 5 _____

Toppling Tree Conundrum

Leonard the lumberjack has to cut down the tall tree on the left. Unfortunately, it's surrounded by smaller trees on each side—and he can't let the big tree drop onto them. How can he discover the height of the tall tree to see if he has enough room?

He knows that:

There are 18 m between the trees.

He is 1.8 m tall.

The small trees' shadows are 1 m long.

The drawing is not to scale!

The small trees are 1.6 m wide.

The small trees are all about 4 m tall.

The tall tree's shadow is 5 m long.

His axe is 1.2 m long.

Moons of Saturn

Saturn has about twenty moons, compared to Earth's one. In the puzzle, find these ten moons: Dione, Enceladus, Hyperion, Lapetus, Janus, Mimas, Phoebe, Rhea, Tethys, Titan and this space probe: Pioneer 11.

The letters left over spell out the name of the scientist who first discovered that Saturn's rings were separate from the planet.

p.s.: One moon appears twice—it orbits Saturn in the opposite direction to all the others.

E	P	I	O	N	E	E	R	11
N	N	A	T	I	T	B	C	H
O	O	C	R	I	M	E	S	L
I	I	T	E	I	I	O	A	A
D	R	A	N	L	M	H	J	P
A	E	H	R	H	A	P	A	E
U	P	Y	G	E	S	D	N	T
S	Y	H	T	E	T	N	U	U
P	H	O	E	B	E	S	S	S

The name of the scientist who first discovered that Saturn's rings were separate from the planet: _____

The name of the moon that appears twice: _____

What's in the Bag? #5

Read the words on the next page. Then match the letters with the correct synonyms in the clues. (You will not use all of the letters.) Put the five clues together and discover what's in the bag!

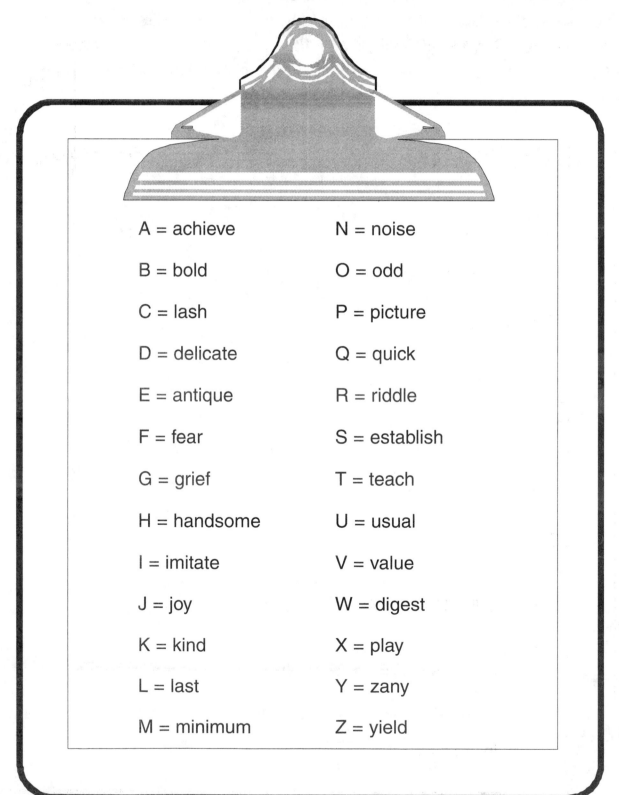

A = achieve	N = noise
B = bold	O = odd
C = lash	P = picture
D = delicate	Q = quick
E = antique	R = riddle
F = fear	S = establish
G = grief	T = teach
H = handsome	U = usual
I = imitate	V = value
J = joy	W = digest
K = kind	X = play
L = last	Y = zany
M = minimum	Z = yield

What's in the Bag? #5 *(cont.)*

Clue 1:

_____   _____   _____   _____   _____   _____

anxiety   final   common   anxiety   anxiety   funny

Clue 2:

_____   _____   _____   _____   _____

eat   lovely   copy   coach   ancient

Clue 3:

_____   _____   _____   _____   _____

form   eat   ancient   ancient   coach

Clue 4:

_____   _____   _____   _____

coach   strange   image   form

Clue 5:

_____   _____   _____   _____   _____

whip   strange   whip   strange   attain

What's in the bag? _____

What's in the Bag? #6

Read the words on the next page. Then match the letters with the correct synonyms in the clues. (You will not use all of the letters.) Put the five clues together and discover what's in the bag!

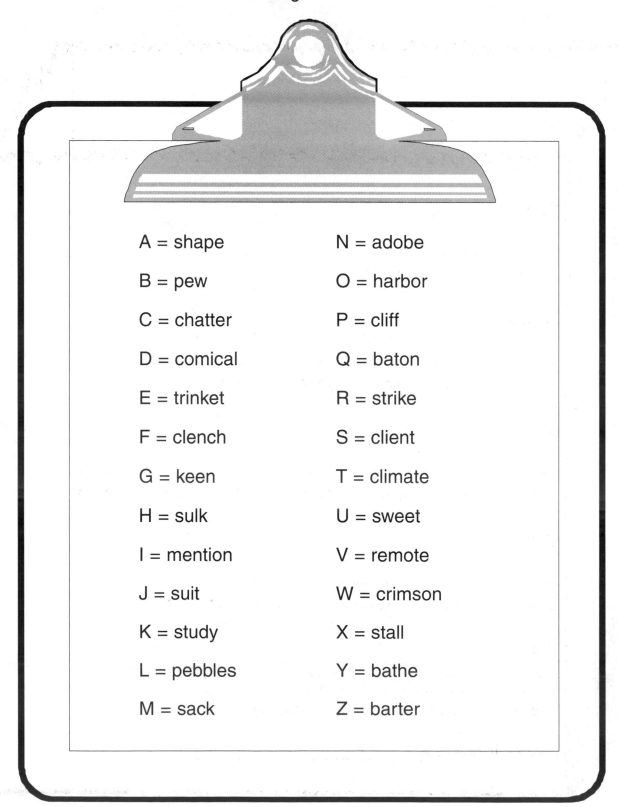

A = shape

B = pew

C = chatter

D = comical

E = trinket

F = clench

G = keen

H = sulk

I = mention

J = suit

K = study

L = pebbles

M = sack

N = adobe

O = harbor

P = cliff

Q = baton

R = strike

S = client

T = climate

U = sweet

V = remote

W = crimson

X = stall

Y = bathe

Z = barter

What's in the Bag? #6 (cont.)

Clue 1:

_____   _____   _____
gravel   form   bench

Clue 2:

_____   _____   _____   _____
weather   cove   cove   gravel

Clue 3:

_____   _____   _____   _____   _____   _____   _____
charm   clay   gravel   form   hit   clever   charm

Clue 4:

_____   _____   _____   _____   _____
grip   cove   jabber   sugary   customer

Clue 5:

_____   _____   _____   _____
gravel   charm   clay   customer

What's in the bag? _____

What's in the Bag? #7

Read the words on the next page. Then match the letters with the correct synonyms in the clues. (You will not use all of the letters.) Put the five clues together and discover what's in the bag!

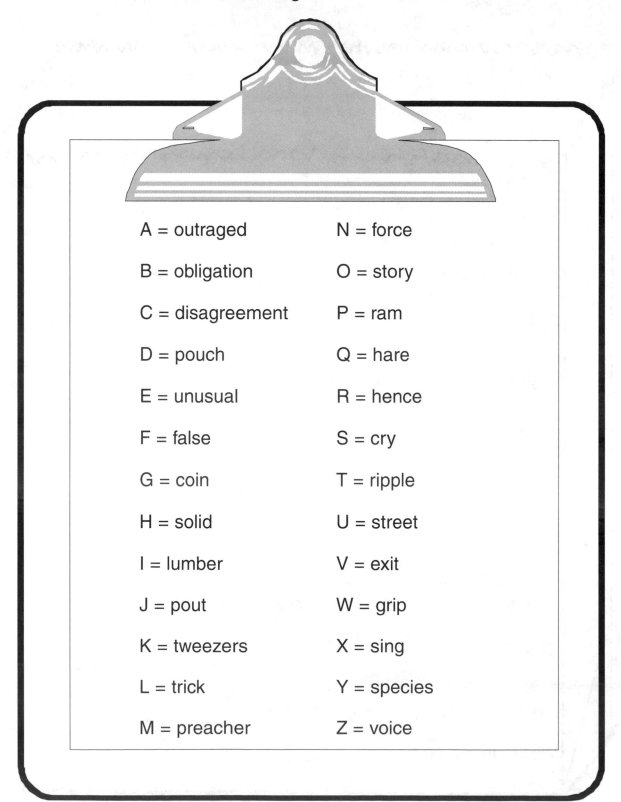

A = outraged

B = obligation

C = disagreement

D = pouch

E = unusual

F = false

G = coin

H = solid

I = lumber

J = pout

K = tweezers

L = trick

M = preacher

N = force

O = story

P = ram

Q = hare

R = hence

S = cry

T = ripple

U = street

V = exit

W = grip

X = sing

Y = species

Z = voice

What's in the Bag? #7 (cont.)

Clue 1:

_____   _____   _____   _____   _____   _____   _____

conflict   tale   tale   tongs   wood   power   token

Clue 2:

_____   _____   _____   _____

firm   unique   thus   duty

Clue 3:

_____   _____   _____   _____   _____   _____

howl   wave   thus   tale   power   token

Clue 4:

_____   _____   _____   _____   _____

grab   firm   wood   wave   unique

Clue 5:

_____   _____   _____   _____

duty   road   prank   duty

What's in the bag? _____

What's in the Bag? #8

Read the words on the next page. Then match the letters with the correct synonyms in the clues. (You will not use all of the letters.) Put the five clues together and discover what's in the bag!

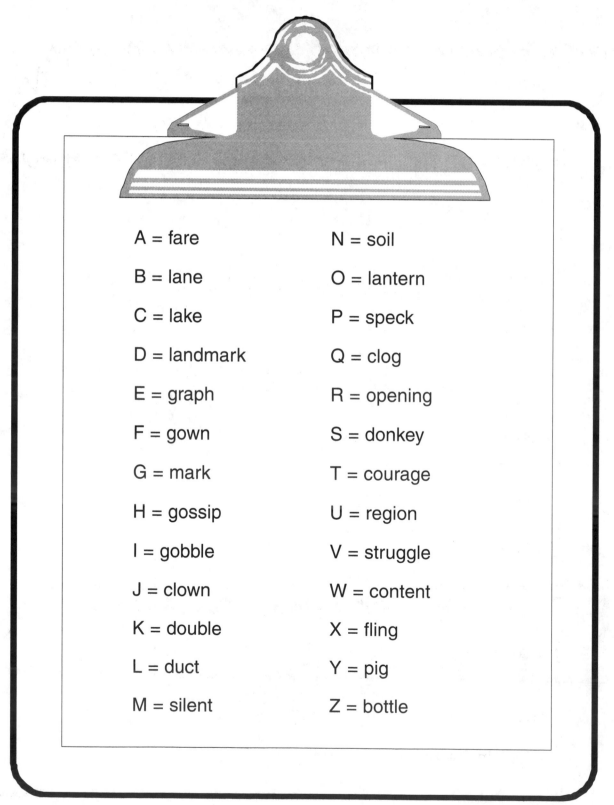

A = fare

B = lane

C = lake

D = landmark

E = graph

F = gown

G = mark

H = gossip

I = gobble

J = clown

K = double

L = duct

M = silent

N = soil

O = lantern

P = speck

Q = clog

R = opening

S = donkey

T = courage

U = region

V = struggle

W = content

X = fling

Y = pig

Z = bottle

210

What's in the Bag? #8 *(cont.)*

Clue 1:

____ ____ ____ ____ ____ ____

lamp　dress　dress　gulp　pond　chart

Clue 2:

____ ____ ____ ____

valor　lamp　lamp　pipe

Clue 3:

____ ____ ____ ____ ____ ____ ____

burro　chart　pond　district　door　chart　burro

Clue 4:

____ ____ ____ ____ ____

pipe　lamp　lamp　spot　burro

Clue 5:

____ ____ ____ ____

satisfied　gulp　door　chart

What's in the bag? _____

Occupation Word Puzzle

If Handel had struck out at being a composer, maybe one of these other jobs in opera may have suited him:

1. a player of a violin shaped instrument with a spike

2. a player of a particular wind instrument

3. a person who plays music

4. a person who ensures pianos are in tune

5. a player of an air-operated keyboard with pipes

6. a female singer with a high voice

7. a person who entertains

8. a wooden flute with a mouthpiece like a whistle.

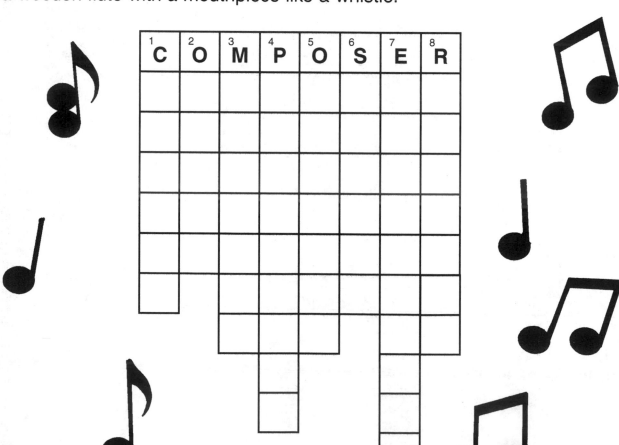

Fast or Slow?

Can you change SLOW into FAST in five tries? You can only change one letter of a word at a time.

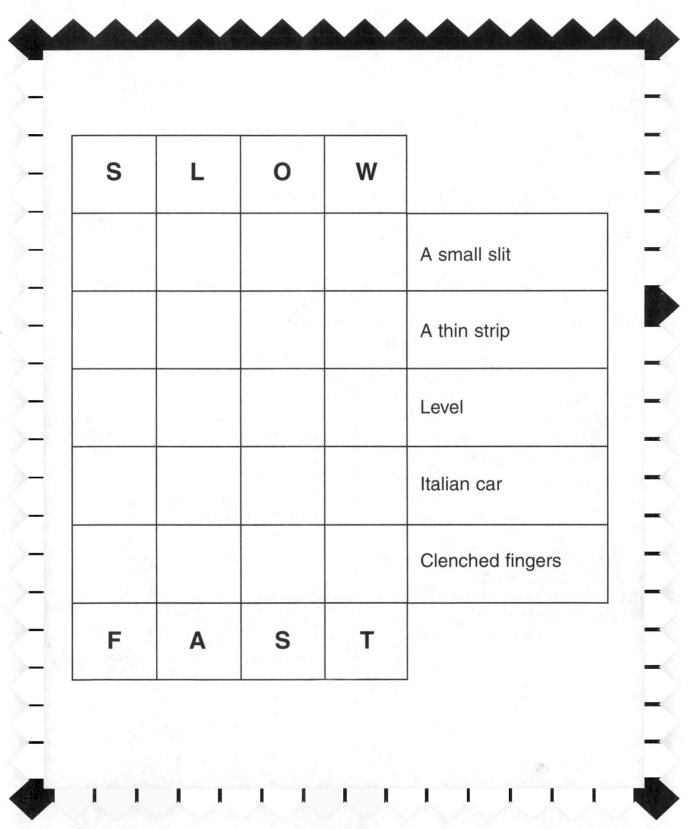

S	L	O	W	
				A small slit
				A thin strip
				Level
				Italian car
				Clenched fingers
F	A	S	T	

In the Middle

It's the middle of the year, and the temperatures are in the mid-teens. You're feeling fair to middling when you get dropped right in the middle of—all these middles.

	Clue:	Answer:
M **I** **D** **D** **L** **E** **+**	between youth and old age	
	the period in history between the Roman Empire and the Renaissance	
	the note on the first ledger line below the staff	
	not rich or poor	
	a cavity essential to hearing	
	the area from Turkey to North Africa	
	a person who buys goods and sells them to shops rather than customers	
	views on issues that are not extreme	
	not large or small	
	a wrestler who weighs 171–192 pounds	

Totem Poles

Can you complete this totem pole puzzle?

					L	1. existing in fact
2. mad or crazy					**I**				
					T	3. win a victory over
4. wagons in single file				**T**			
					L	5. a book of instructions
6. protection for travelers				**E**				
				B	7. to move upwards
8. name for Native American				**I**		
					G	9. to adjust so movements occur in proper sequence
10. four-legged mammals used in warfare				**H**			
			O	11. one of Custer's officers
12. a large stream			**R**			
				N	13. a large flat area of land

From Traitor To Patriot

A Traitor is only one letter away from a Patriot. Use the clues to work out these words.

Traitor	−	R	+	P	=	one who loves and defends his or her country	Patriot
		T		P		an airfield with control tower and hangers	
		I		C		a vehicle with large wheels used in farming	
		O		E		more worn and torn	
		T,R		C,P		orange-colored fruit	
		T,R		Y,P		trimming shrubs or trees into shapes	

George Giraffe

By the time you complete this word puzzle (George has filled in some letters for you), you'll know all about giraffes! You may need to do some research to complete this puzzle.

1. Giraffes have an excellent sense of…
2. Number of neck vertebrae
3. The giraffe's chief predator
4. Giraffes live south of this desert.
5. The giraffe's _____ is long and flexible.
6. Captive giraffes can live up to 36 _____.
7. Giraffes may need to _____ if their food source depletes.
8. The giraffe's favorite tree
9. Older giraffes are a darker _____.
10. The giraffe belongs to this group of animals.
11. Giraffes bear only one _____ at a time.
12. Male giraffes use their long necks to _____.
13. Giraffes live in groups called _____.

Zip It Up!

Put zip in your day—and your vocabulary. All the following words have a "zip" in them somewhere. Use the clues to work out the whole word.

1. A type of monkey _____

2. Conduct as a citizen _____

3. A city in east central Germany_____

4. A sweet made with almond paste _____

5. Spectacles clipped to the nose by a spring_____

6. Italian open pie _____

7. Method of playing a stringed instrument by plucking_____

8. Award for victory in a contest_____

9. A mystery, or bewildering_____

10. A quadrilateral with only one pair of opposite sides parallel _____

11. A large dirigible balloon _____

12. An American post-code _____

#										
1		I		P			Z			
2			I	Z					P	
3			P	Z	I					
4			Z	I	P					
5	P	I						Z		
6	P	I		Z						
7	P			Z	I					
8	P		I	Z						
9	P			Z		I				
10			P		Z		I			
11	Z			P			I			
12	Z	I	P							

218

Bridge Word Search

Find these bridges in the word search below. The leftover letters spell out the name of an unusual bridge in the United States.

Akashi Kaikyo	moveable bridge
arch	pontoon
cantilever	span
Clifton	support
Commonwealth Bridge	suspension
Golden Gate	Sydney Harbour Bridge
Humber	Tasman
London Bridge	Tower Bridge
Mackinac	Victoria Bridge

```
E G D I R B H T L A E W N O M M O C A N T I L E V E R C H E
S Y D N E Y H A R B O U R B R I D G E G D I R B N O D N O L
T A S M A N E G D I R B A I R O T C I V N O I S N E P S U S
S A E G D I R B E L B A V O M E G D I R B R E W O T H C R A
A K A S H I K A I K Y O          E T A G N E D L O G P
M A C K I N A C E A K            N O T F I L C E B A
P O N T O O N A P S              S U P P O R T Y B
H U M B E R R I D                G E T U N N E L
```

The name of the unusual bridge in the United States:

_____.

Jumbo Elephants

Test your "jumbo" knowledge here! When you've completed all the horizontal words, the central vertical word spells out an alternative name for an elephant.

1. The largest land animal

2. Smaller of the two types of elephants

3. Larger of the two types of elephants—its ears look like a map of its home

4. The elephant's ancient hairy ancestor

5. Flesh-eating mammal that preys on elephant calves (baby elephants)

6. An extinct type of elephant

7. To search for food

8. A group of elephants

9. The elephant is this type of animal

Rods

Here are seven words with "rod" in them—can you find what they are?

R O D + _____ =

to poke	
stepped	
a car modified for speed	
a rod inside an engine	
a rod for finding water	
a rod that protects a building from lightning	
a rod between 1 cm and 10 cm used in math	

Jules Verne Acrostic

The missing words come from titles of Jules Verne's novels, or predictions he made about the future.

1. _____ to the Center of the Earth

2. Clipper of the _____

3. Flying machine with rotating wings

4. Around the World in _____ Days

5. The Mysterious_____

6. Animated photographs

7. 20,000 _____ Under the Sea

8. A submersible boat

9. Round the_____

10. From the _____ to the Moon

Tammy's Tattoos

Tammy the tattoo artist will only do tattoos of objects that have the word tattoo in them. Her range, to say the least, is limited. What can she draw? Use the letters of the word "tattoo" and combine them with the letters in the second column. Use the clues to help you solve the words.

T A T T O O	+ HOP	A cooked spud	
	+ CILN	Small rabbit	
	+ EHPS	Paste for cleaning teeth	
	+ EEPSW	Type of yam	
	+ HPS	Photocopy	
	+ DDEPS	Amphibian with spots	
	+ EEMR	South American plant that looks like a tomato	

Tipperary

What can you find in Tipperary, the name of a town in Ireland?

How many words of at least four letters can you make from "Tipperary"? Oh, and they have to start with a T . . . .

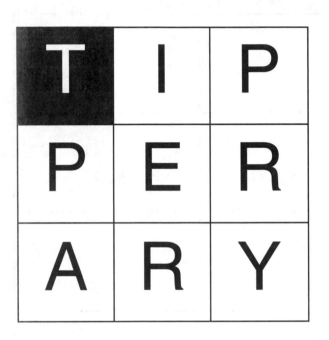

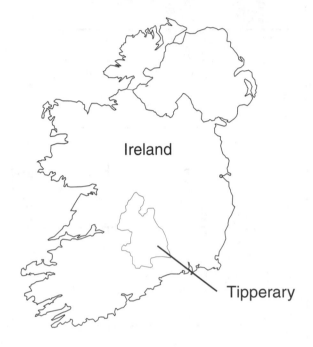

Ireland

Tipperary

_____ _____ _____ _____

_____ _____ _____ _____

_____ _____ _____ _____

_____ _____ _____ _____

_____ _____ _____ _____

E's Front and Back

Use the clues to fill in the blanks in the following words. All the words both begin and end with the letter **e**.

1.	e ___ ___ ___ ___ ___ e	to do
2.	e ___ ___ ___ ___ ___ e	make higher
3.	e ___ ___ e	comfort
4.	e ___ ___ ___ e	national bird
5.	e ___ ___ ___ ___ ___ ___ e	guess
6.	e ___ ___ ___ ___ ___ ___ e	teachers do this
7.	e ___ ___ ___ ___ ___ ___ e	a letter goes in one
8.	e ___ ___ ___ ___ ___ ___ e	data or proof
9.	e ___ ___ ___ e	send away
10.	e ___ e	female sheep
11.	e ___ ___ ___ ___ ___ ___ e	leave
12.	e ___ ___ ___ ___ ___ e	to check
13.	e ___ ___ ___ ___ ___ ___ ___ e	disappear
14.	e ___ ___ ___ ___ ___ ___ e	workout
15.	e ___ ___ ___ ___ ___ ___ ___ e	cheer up or cheer on
16.	e ___ ___ ___ ___ ___ ___ e	administrator
17.	e ___ ___ ___ ___ e	breathe out
18.	e ___ ___ ___ ___ e	get free
19.	e ___ ___ ___ ___ e	lure
20.	e ___ ___ ___ ___ ___ ___ ___ e	to free from oppression

Letter Answers

Use one or two letters of the alphabet to respond to each of the clues. The first
one has been done for you.

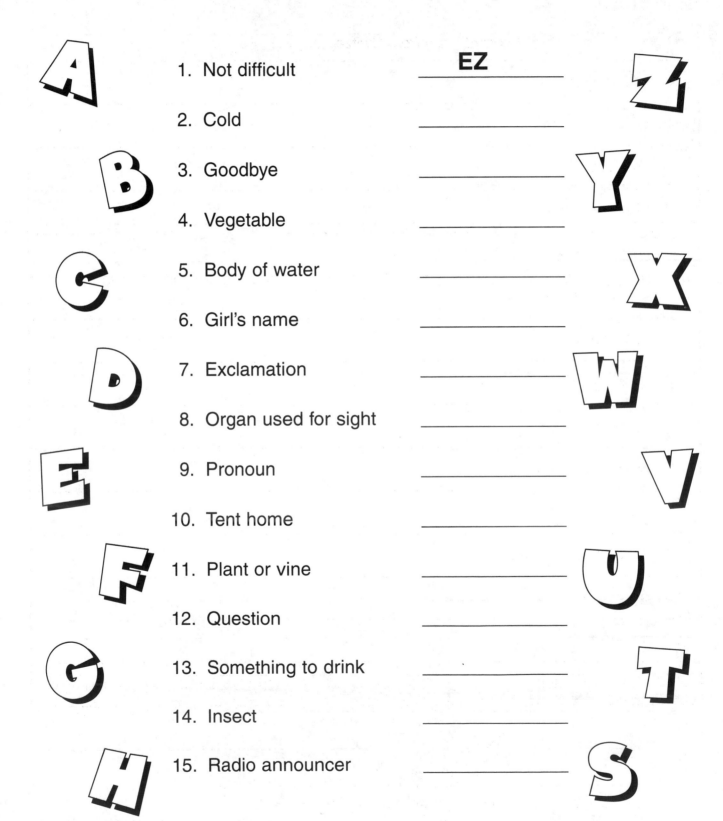

1. Not difficult   **EZ** _____

2. Cold   _____

3. Goodbye   _____

4. Vegetable   _____

5. Body of water   _____

6. Girl's name   _____

7. Exclamation   _____

8. Organ used for sight   _____

9. Pronoun   _____

10. Tent home   _____

11. Plant or vine   _____

12. Question   _____

13. Something to drink   _____

14. Insect   _____

15. Radio announcer   _____

Rhyming Word Pairs

Find an adjective that rhymes with a noun so that the two words together have about the same meaning as the phrase that is given. An example has been done for you.

Example: girl from Switzerland = Swiss miss

1. ailing William =	
2. mischievous boy =	
3. unhappy friend =	
4. bashful insect =	
5. fiesty primate =	
6. overweight referee =	
7. soft young dog =	
8. unhappy father =	
9. soaked dog =	
10. watered-down red juice =	
11. reliable Theodore =	
12. flower that is messy =	
13. tiny bug =	
14. ill hen =	
15. smart instrument =	

Word Chains

To make a word chain, each new word must begin with the last letter of the previous word. For example, if the category is Famous Americans, a possible word chain would be the following: George Bush—Herbert Hoover—Ronald Reagan, etc. This can be adapted to any area of study or played in teams, each team taking turns adding to the chain.

Countries	Proper Nouns	Foods
Chile	Betsy Ross	hot dog
England	Salt Lake City	green bean

Coded Message

Circle the correct letter for each problem below. Then, take the circled letter and put it in the corresponding blank in order to reveal a famous saying.

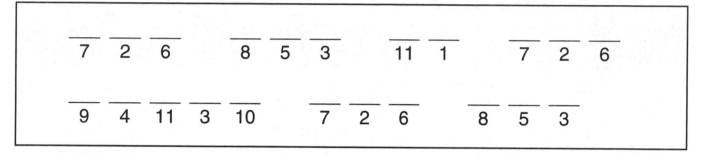

1. If man walked on the moon in 1492, circle S. If not, circle F.

2. If a prairie dog is a dog, circle K. If it is a rodent, circle O.

3. _____ If your father's sister is your aunt, circle N. If not, circle A.

4. If 6 x 9 = 55, circle M. If not, circle H.

5. If antonyms are words that mean the opposite of one another, circle A. If not, circle L.

6. _____ If Brazil is a country in Europe, circle K. If not, circle U.

7. If the capital of Illinois is Springfield, circle Y. If not circle, U.

8. If the trumpet is a woodwind instrument, circle Z. If not, circle C.

9. If Charles Dickens wrote David Copperfield, circle T. If not, circle W.

10. If a telescope is used to view things far away, circle K. If not, circle M.

11. If the Statue of Liberty is located in Washington, D.C., circle E. If not, circle I.

The Wheel

1. The wheel was first invented in Sumer about 3500 B.C. By about 3250 B.C., the first wheeled vehicles were used there. How do you think the idea of the wheel might first have come to the Sumerians? Write your thoughts here:

   _____

   _____

2. How might the first wheels have been made?

   _____

   _____

3. List the improvements made by the wheel for these people in the chart below.

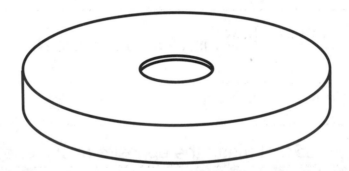

Rulers	Traders	Farmers	(you choose)

Heroes

Brainstorm: What makes a person a hero? List as many ideas as you can think of.

Can you write a definition of a hero?

_____

_____

_____

Are there any particular occupations from which heroes emerge? Why do you think this is so?

_____

_____

_____

_____

More Heroes

List all the ways that people in the following occupations could be heroes:

a. teachers _____

_____

_____

b. plumbers _____

_____

_____

c. bank tellers _____

_____

_____

d. bus drivers _____

_____

_____

e. doctors _____

_____

_____

f. nurses _____

_____

_____

g. students _____

_____

_____

Louis Braille's Code

(Born January 4, 1809)

Louis Braille was a Frenchman who invented a raised dot writing system for the blind. A special typewriter presses against paper to form the different dot sequences.

Use the Braille letter dot code to write and read the messages.

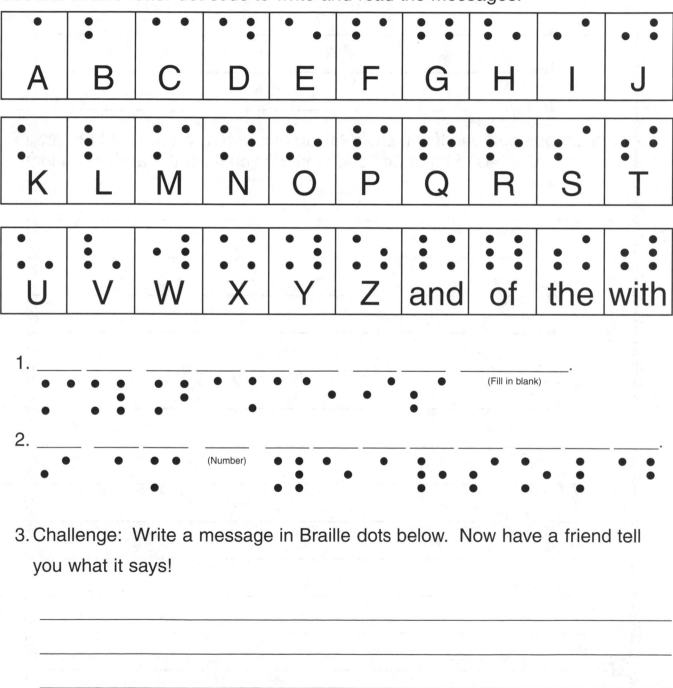

1. _____ _____ _____ _____ _____.
                                                                    (Fill in blank)

2. _____ _____ _____ _____ _____ _____ _____.
              (Number)

3. Challenge: Write a message in Braille dots below. Now have a friend tell you what it says!

_____

_____

_____

_____

Famous People

The answer is "fame."

List 5 questions.

1. _____

2. _____

3. _____

4. _____

5. _____

Choose a famous person. If you could talk to him or her, what would be three questions you would ask him or her, and what do you think the answers might be?

1. _____

_____

_____

_____

2. _____

_____

_____

_____

3. _____

_____

_____

_____

Problems and Solutions

Select three major problems facing America today.

1. _____

   _____

   _____

2. _____

   _____

   _____

3. _____

   _____

   _____

What are your solutions?

1. _____

   _____

   _____

2. _____

   _____

   _____

3. _____

   _____

   _____

Great Ideas!

List all the ways you can celebrate a holiday.

_____

_____

_____

_____

_____

Suggest different ways that children can amuse themselves
when they feel bored.

_____

_____

_____

_____

How many different reasons can you think of why you might
not be able to close the front door?

_____

_____

_____

_____

_____

Greetings!

List all the different ways that you can think of to greet people. You can show your answers with words and pictures.

Koalas

Make the following statements into questions.

━━━━━━━━━━━━━━━━━ **Factual** ━━━━━━━━━━━━━━━━━

1. Koalas, kangaroos, dolphins, dogs, and humans are all types of mammals.

_____

_____

_____

━━━━━━━━━━━━━━━━━ **Inferential** ━━━━━━━━━━━━━━━━━

2. With more houses being built and more families moving into the area, more domestic animals will be a part of a koala's habitat.

_____

_____

_____

━━━━━━━━━━━━━━━━━ **Critical** ━━━━━━━━━━━━━━━━━

3. I think that we need to stop allowing houses to be built in the habitat of koalas.

_____

_____

_____

━━━━━━━━━━━━━━━━━ **Creative** ━━━━━━━━━━━━━━━━━

4. Sometimes a koala can "fly" from a limb of one tree to a limb of another tree by flapping its front legs very quickly.

_____

_____

_____

Traveling Overseas

1. List the things you would need to organize before leaving your home to go on an overseas trip.

   _____

   _____

   _____

2. Where would you locate information about the length and cost of an overseas trip?

   _____

   _____

   _____

3. What are some of the problems you could encounter? How would you avoid these problems?

Problem	How to avoid it

A Funny Speech

Your favorite funny character has been asked to give a talk at your school. Write out his/her speech.

_____

_____

_____

_____

_____

_____

_____

_____

_____

_____

_____

_____

_____

Future of America

On a seperate sheet of paper, write a brief time line of some of the changes that have taken place in your lifetime.

Illustrate one of the changes in a cartoon strip.

1.	2.	3.
4.	5.	6.
7.	8.	9.

The Importance of Coins

Business has been carried on using a trading or bartering system for many hundreds of years. Coinage was introduced in Persia about 500 B.C. and in China about 220 B.C. How would this have changed the daily activities of the traders and other business people?

_____

_____

_____

_____

_____

_____

_____

_____

_____

_____

_____

_____

Non-Human Hero

Write a story where a non-human becomes a hero.

New-Age Poem

Write a poem depicting life in the year 2500.

Brainstorming About Food

What is food? _____

_____

_____

_____

_____

_____

_____

Who needs food? _____

_____

_____

_____

_____

_____

_____

Why do we need food? _____

_____

_____

_____

_____

_____

_____

What is your favorite food? Describe this food in 20 words.

_____   _____   _____   _____

_____   _____   _____   _____

_____   _____   _____   _____

_____   _____   _____   _____

_____   _____   _____   _____

food Groups

Give examples of common foods in each group. Combine at least one food from each group to make a balanced meal. Describe this meal and draw a picture of it.

Common foods in each group:

_____

_____

_____

_____

_____

_____

Described a balanced meal:

_____

_____

_____

_____

_____

_____

Draw this meal:

Math Likes

What do you like about mathematics? Why?

_____

_____

_____

_____

Name 10 fun things you can do that use math.

1. _____   6. _____

2. _____   7. _____

3. _____   8. _____

4. _____   9. _____

5. _____   10. _____

Pick one of these things and write about it.

_____

_____

_____

_____

_____

_____

Working Math

List as many different people as you can who use math every day in their professions.

Choose two of these people.

_____ _____

Write down five questions to ask these people about how they use math in their professions.

1. _____

2. _____

3. _____

4. _____

5. _____

Survival

What does "survival" mean?

_____

_____

_____

_____

What do I need to survive?

_____

_____

_____

_____

How do I ensure that I have everything I need to survive?

_____

_____

_____

_____

If I had to do without something to survive, what would it be?

_____

If I could add another element to my needs for survival, what would it be?

_____

_____

_____

Calculating

Draw a mathematical calculator like the one you use at school.

Write and practice a short speech explaining how to use the calculator to a younger student at your school.

Designing an Exhibition

You have been asked to design a new exhibit for the local museum containing artifacts found during the excavations of a city believed to be over 2,000 years old. How would you choose what to display and the information provided for visitors? Write down your findings and begin your preliminary sketches of the exhibit. Include some drawings of artifacts that will be on display.

List of artifacts chosen for display	Information about the artifacts

Plan of display

Inventions

1. Choose an invention that you would like to investigate. The invention I will investigate is _____.

2. Write down five things that you already know about this invention.

   a. _____

   b. _____

   c. _____

   d. _____

   e. _____

3. Write down four things that you would like to know about this invention.

   a. _____

   b. _____

   c. _____

   d. _____

4. Change one component in this invention. What effect would this have?

The component I changed . . .	How it will work now . . .
_____	_____
_____	_____
_____	_____
_____	_____
What the new component looks like . . .	**Did I improve the invention? . . .**
_____	_____
_____	_____
_____	_____

I'm a Hero!

Imagine you have the opportunity to become a hero.

Choose one of these scenarios:
- a fire
- an accident
- a storm

Display your heroic feats in this cartoon strip.

1.	2.	3.
4.	**5.**	**6.**
7.	**8.**	**9.**

Poem Puzzle

Robinson Crusoe would never have survived without help—from whom?

_____

Use the clues below to answer the question.

1. My first is in maroon but not in lagoon. _____

2. My second is in palm but not helm. _____

3. My third is in land and also in sand. _____

4. My fourth is in fir but not elm. _____

5. My fifth is in rifle but nowhere in gun. _____

6. My sixth is in sink but not sunk. _____

7. My seventh's in danger and hazard, not axe! _____

8. My eighth is in water and wax. _____

9. My last is in years, and every and why— _____

My all's a beloved friend. (Spell out the letters from the first three clues.)

_____

I'm named for the day that we met on the beach and the day that the working week ends. (Spell out the letters from clues four through nine.)

_____

Blood Donors

Alan, Chris, and Brad visit the blood bank. They fill out their details and list their professions (not necessarily in order) as scientist, sprinter, and secretary. Their blood types are tested and one is type A, one is type B, and one is type O. If you know that:

1) Brad was ahead of the secretary in the line and behind Chris.

2) Chris has type B blood, but the sprinter has A.

Can you work out each donor's profession and blood type?

	Secretary	Sprinter	Scientist	A	O	B
Alan						
Brad						
Chris						

Alan: _____

Brad: _____

Chris: _____

Hidden Meanings

Explain the meaning of each box.

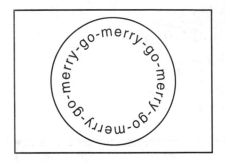

1. _____

| **E   EEE EEEE EEEE** (LIFE pattern) |

2. _____

MCE
MCE
MCE

3. _____

YOUR
P_aA_nN_tT_sS

4. _____

〈   〉
A

5. _____

CYCLE
CYCLE
CYCLE

6. _____

STAND
———
I

7. _____

R
ROAD
A
D

8. _____

S
B
M
U
H
T

9. _____

Once
———
A Time

10. _____

GESG

11. _____

You/Just/Me

12. _____

10 Questions

Write a question for each of the following answers.

1. **Question:** _____

   Answer: Saturn

2. **Question:** _____

   Answer: Cat

3. **Question:** _____

   Answer: Train

4. **Question:** _____

   Answer: 18

5. **Question:** _____

   Answer: Mozart

6. **Question:** _____

   Answer: Atlantic Ocean

7. **Question:** _____

   Answer: Earthquake

8. **Question:** _____

   Answer: 22

9. **Question:** _____

   Answer: Thanksgiving

10. **Question:** _____

    Answer: Atlas

Softball Lineup

All nine players on the Tiger softball team are sitting on the bench in their batting order. Using the clues below, find their batting order. Record their batting order by putting an **X** in the correct box.

1. Jane is batting fifth, and Daisy will bat some time before Carrie.

2. Joanne sits between Daisy and Gertie, and Annie is to the right of Jane.

3. Gertie bats after Joanne but before Annie.

4. Penny sits next to Carrie.

5. Carrie and Tammy are at each end of the bench.

	1	2	3	4	5	6	7	8	9
Jane									
Daisy									
Carrie									
Joanne									
Gertie									
Annie									
Penny									
Tammy									
Lindsey									

Six Words

Write as many sentences as you can, using the following words:

gumball, serious, shrieking, follow, happy, day

Can you write a sentence that includes all the words?

_____

_____

_____

_____

_____

_____

_____

_____

_____

_____

_____

_____

_____

_____

_____

_____

_____

Computer Complaints

If computers could talk, what do you think would be the 10 major complaints they would have?

_____

_____

_____

_____

_____

_____

_____

_____

_____

_____

_____

_____

_____

_____

_____

Umbrelon

Choose two unrelated objects, such as a melon and an umbrella, and combine them. Choose a name for the new object, and then list what the qualities of the object are, and what the object could be used for. Draw the new object.

 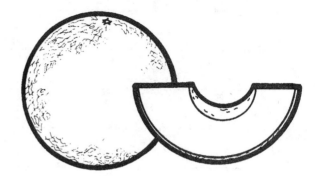

Square Eggs!

Visualize a square egg. Explain in detail how you think this egg could be used, and what might be the advantages and disadvantages of its shape.

_____

_____

_____

_____

_____

_____

_____

_____

_____

_____

_____

_____

_____

_____

_____

_____

_____

Out in Space!

List as many objects as you can think of that you would find in outer space. Think of ways to group or categorize the objects, and give each category or group a label.

List:

Items listed under their categories:

What Do You Expect?

Design a questionnaire to predict what American people expect of the future.

What Could This Be?

List two objects or images that each drawing could be.

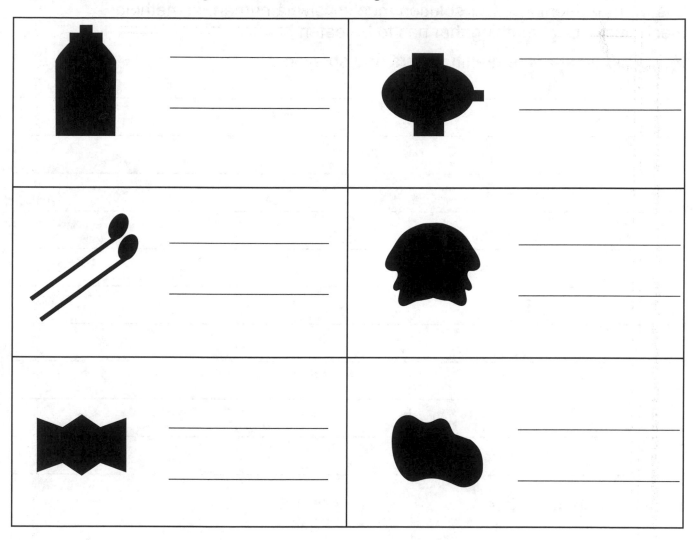

Draw one of your own and have a friend guess what it is.

Clean the Graffiti

Your school has a terrible problem with graffiti. Think of ways that you can stop this from happening. Your solution must involve a human, something mechanical, or something that has to be eaten.

How will you stop the graffiti writers and sprayers?

_____

_____

_____

_____

_____

_____

_____

_____

_____

Draw your solution here.

Come and Play

Imagine you are in a junkyard. There are old tires, ladders with missing rungs, empty paint tins, boxes, ropes, old cupboards, etc.

Think about how you might use these items to design a safe playground for a number of students. Think about what other recycled items you would like to add. Write your ideas here.

_____

_____

_____

_____

_____

_____

_____

_____

_____

Draw a map of your new playground in the space below, labeling its different parts.

Brushing Plus . . .

Create an improved toothbrush. Make sure that for each change that is made, there is a clear explanation. You could use the **BAR** strategy to help you consider how different features could be improved.

B = make it **bigger**

A = **add** something

R = **remove** something and **replace** it with something else

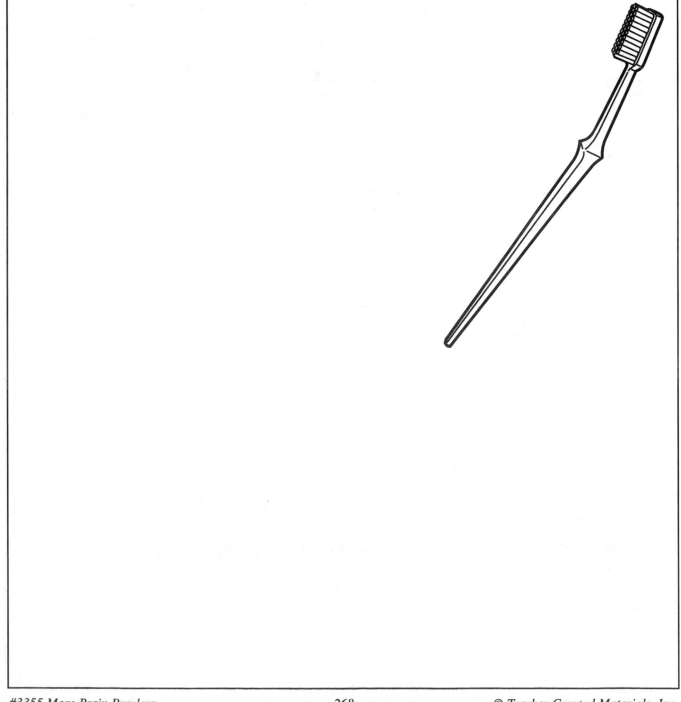

Egyptian Writing

If you visit Egypt you may find some very old writing on some walls. Here is what some of the symbols mean:

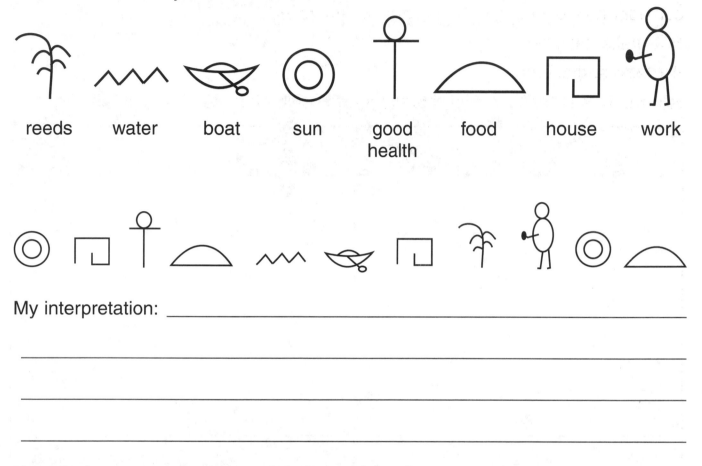

reeds   water   boat   sun   good health   food   house   work

My interpretation: _____

_____

_____

_____

Now design your own picture alphabet which tells a story about life in ancient Egypt and the building of the Great Pyramid.

My Picture Alphabet Symbols

My Story

City of the Future

1. Imagine that you could design a model of a **City of the Future** which will have no pollution problems.

2. Explain how you would solve each of the following potential pollution problems in your city.

My **City of the Future** would be called: _____

Potential Problem	Solution
household waste	
polluted drinking water	
air pollution from cars	
air pollution from factories	
noise pollution from cars and planes	

Pollution

Read each statement below and decide if you agree or disagree. Place a mark on the line to show how you feel. Explain why you made this choice.

1. Pollution is a necessary part of modern life.

   |———————————————————————————————|

   Agree   Disagree

   Justification: _____

2. Household waste can easily be reduced.

   |———————————————————————————————|

   Agree   Disagree

   Justification: _____

3. Pollution is not a problem in our local environment.

   |———————————————————————————————|

   Agree   Disagree

   Justification: _____

4. The media exaggerates pollution problems.

   |———————————————————————————————|

   Agree   Disagree

   Justification: _____

5. All countries should use nuclear power because it produces cheap electricity.

   |———————————————————————————————|

   Agree   Disagree

   Justification: _____

Explanations

Bright purple snow is falling! Give five possible explanations for this.

1. _____
   _____

2. _____
   _____

3. _____
   _____

4. _____
   _____

5. _____
   _____

Draw a picture showing how people might react to seeing purple snow.

Survival Skills

You and a friend have been shipwrecked on a deserted island. The ship you were on has sunk in 10 yards of water not far from the shore. All that you could salvage from the ship was:

- a piece of rope
- a sheet from one of the bunks
- a bucket

You must both survive until the next ship passes in 30 days.

Describe what you would do to survive.

_____

_____

_____

_____

_____

_____

_____

_____

Invent something that would help you to attract the attention of the passing ship. Describe and illustrate how this will help you.

_____

_____

_____

_____

_____

_____

_____

Planning a Dinner Menu

How many of your favorite foods originated in another country? Complete this table. Choose four more countries to add to the table.

Country	Name of Dish	Main Ingredients
Italy		
Spain		
China		
India		
France		
Japan		
Mexico		

Bug Fan Club

First, think of your favorite insect. Write it here: _____

Write five questions that you would ask a bug expert in order to gain more information about this insect.

_____

_____

_____

_____

_____

List all the words you can think of that would describe this insect. Be as creative and thorough as you can.

_____

_____

_____

_____

_____

Draw your insect surrounded by these words.

Solar Systems

On the chart below all the planets in our solar system are listed in order of their proximity to the sun. Fill in the squares with Yes or No. Some of the headings have been filled in for you. Use your own ideas for the rest.

Planet	Small	Round	Has moons		
Mercury					
Venus					
Earth					
Mars					
Jupiter					
Saturn					
Uranus					
Neptune					
Pluto					

What do all the planets have in common? _____

_____

In what ways are the planets different? _____

_____

What do Mercury, Venus, and Pluto have in common? _____

_____

List the planets according to their size. _____

_____

Come to My Party!

Make up a party list of your five favorite humorous characters. Design some party games they might like to play.

Cartoon Hero

Who is your favorite cartoon hero? Draw him/her in action.

Uniforms

What are uniforms? _____

Name six groups of people who wear uniforms.

_____

_____

_____

_____

_____

Why do these people wear uniforms?

_____

_____

_____

_____

_____

If you could design your own uniform, what would it look like? Draw a picture of it below and describe your design.

_____

_____

_____

_____

Protective Clothing

Illustrate and label 10 articles of clothing worn as protection in a work situation. Which occupations require wearing these clothes?

_____	_____	_____	_____	_____
_____	_____	_____	_____	_____

Progress Chart

Page	Title	Date	Completed

Progress Chart *(cont.)*

Page	Title	Date	Completed

Progress Chart *(cont.)*

Page	Title	Date	Completed

Progress Chart *(cont.)*

Page	Title	Date	Completed

Progress Chart (cont.)

Page	Title	Date	Completed

Progress Chart *(cont.)*

Page	Title	Date	Completed

Progress Chart *(cont.)*

Page	Title	Date	Completed

Progress Chart *(cont.)*

Page	Title	Date	Completed

Answer Key

Page 15 What Makes 12?
Answers will vary.

Page 16 Patterns

Page 17 Standard Measurements
Answers will vary.

Page 18 Scaling Scales
Answers will vary.

Page 19 John, Jack, and the Nuggets
Start at the arrow. Remember that the nuggets are taken, so they aren't counted on the second round.

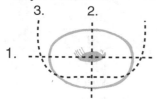

Page 20 Tortoise Trails
C

Page 21 House Math
That Jack built.

Page 22 Invasion: Earth!
Mars at its closest distance is 51 million km. The martians are 1 million km short.

Page 23 Door-to-Door
Down the first column, up the second, and down the third.

Page 24 Doughnut Decision
Slice in half across the hole, slice in quarters across the hole, and slice into eighths horizontally to the hole.

Page 25 Exam Time
Cara = A, Lucy = B, Martin = C, Gwen = C-, Donald = D.

Page 26 Proverbial Codes
1. Look before you leap.
2. Never put off until tomorrow what can be done today.
3. A friend in need is a friend indeed.
4. The early bird catches the worm.
5. All that glitters is not gold.
6. Don't cry over spilled milk.
7. You never know what you can do until you try.
8. Make yourself necessary to someone.

Page 27 Word Problems
1. $.94
2. $.84, $.08
3. 2792 pennies

Page 28 Word Problems (cont.)
4. 30,251 miles
5. 483 marbles
6. 38,404 people

Page 29 Word Problems (cont.)
7. $3.60
8. $14.35
9. 84 socks
10. 214 rocks

Page 30 Time
Answers will vary.

Page 31 Frog Hop!
Skippy 5.7m

Page 32 Prime Time

Answer Key *(cont.)*

Page 33 Word Stair Puzzle

1. eat	6. react	11. mink
2. tow	7. task	12. king
3. wear	8. knife	13. girl
4. road	9. egg	
5. deer	10. germ	

Page 34 Light Bulb Word Search

How many can you afford?

Page 35 Keyboarding

flags, flash, flask

Dvorak keyboard: Andes, audio, aunts, dates, deans, death, donut, duets, hands, hated, haunt, hints, hosed, hunts, ideas, noted, saint, shade, shine, shone, shout, sited, sound, stain, stand, stone, those, unite (to name a few!)

Page 36 Pinocchio

Chin, chip, chop, Chopin, cinch, coin, con, conch, coop, cop, hip, hoop, hop, icon, inch, nip, phonic, picnic, pin, pinch, Pinocchio, poncho, pooch

Page 37 Oyster Antics

necklace

Page 38 Word Twins

Aches and pains, again and again, alive and kicking, bacon and eggs, bells and whistles, bits and pieces, crackers and cheese, cut and paste, fair and square, fish and chips, night and day, nuts and bolts, odds and ends, rock and roll, salt and pepper, stars and stripes, thick and thin

Page 39 Winnie-the-Pooh Word Puzzle

1. Wol
2. Tigger
3. Kanga
4. Sanders
5. Rabbit
6. Eeyore
7. Christopher
8. honey
9. acre
10. piglet
11. owl
12. Robin
13. howse

Page 40 Cornflake Word Chase

Can, car, café, cake, calf, cane, care, clan, coal, cola, cone, core, cork, corn, canoe, carol, clank, clean, clear, clerk, cloak, clone, coral, crane, crank, creak, croak, cornea

Page 41 Reading Scramble

1. book
2. library
3. read
4. words
5. picture
6. print
7. page
8. author
9. artist
10. type
11. story
12. plot
13. cover
14. character
15. illustration

Page 42 Alphabetical Order

1. broom
2. chain
3. drum
4. egg
5. flower
6. hand
7. jar
8. letter
9. music
10. number
11. potato
12. star
13. table
14. umbrella
15. whale
16. yellow

Page 43 Five-Letter Words

1. large	6. thief	11. under
2. learn	7. earth	12. allow
3. story	8. price	13. bring
4. right	9. write	14. happy
5. start	10. hurry	15. shout

Answer Key (cont.)

Page 44 The Great Outdoors

Answers will vary.

Page 45 Word Pairs

1. huff
2. tar
3. cats
4. nook
5. thick
6. mix
7. tooth/hammer
8. cream
9. fine
10. back
11. scream
12. sticks
13. up
14. dollars
15. peaches
16. law
17. rise
18. war
19. in
20. black
21. prim
22. body/heart
23. silk
24. hook
25. pen/pencil

Page 46–Page 55

Answers will vary.

Page 56 The Handy Dandy Fairy Tale Writer

Answers will vary.
1. Three Little Pigs
2. Red Riding Hood
3. Rumpelstiltskin
4. Jack and the Beanstalk
5. The Three Billy Goats Gruff

Page 57–Page 71

Answers will vary.

Page 72 Talking About Birds

1. turkeys, chickens, ducks, geese
2. because they have webbed feet

Page 73–Page 80

Answers will vary.

Page 81 Spot the Forgery

nails, frame, sky, tree, badge, hair, shirt, expression, freckles, land/water

Page 82 Railway Words

1. railway crossing
2. a train in the station
3. round trip ticket
4. railway line

Page 83 Pipeline Puzzle

It comes out at tap two.

Page 84 To Bee or Not to Bee . . .

Flower pot 1

Page 85 Lightning Rod

B is attached to D, A is flying free, and Ben is holding onto C.

Page 86 Amazing!

It is a trick puzzle. Try going around the outside.

Page 87 Colorful Language

1. red
2. yellow
3. green
4. white
5. black
6. pink
7. red
8. orange

Page 88 Assembly Line Blues

A. missing rear-view mirror
B. missing turn signal lights
C. missing windshield wiper
D. no back window
E. no headlights

Page 89 How Amazing!

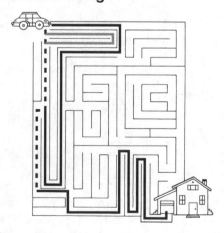

Page 90 Homes

1. Marla—pink
2. Pepper—red
3. Rosa—yellow

Page 91 In the Library

Answers will vary.

Answer Key (cont.)

Page 92 Which One Does Not Belong?
1. June—months that end in -er/or are consecutive
2. glove—footwear
3. notebook—writing tools
4. page—royalty/queen
5. Rich—form of Robert
6. carnation—wood
7. layer cake—cookies
8. nephew—females
9. television—machines for talking into
10. flower—furniture
11. grapefruit—melons
12. strange—noises
13. elephant—large cats
14. lightbulb—tools
15. colon—end punctuation

Page 93 All Alike
1. types of dance
2. sports
3. flowers
4. large cats
5. desserts/sweets
6. tools
7. moods
8. gemstones
9. dairy products
10. one
11. things that are round
12. air transportation
13. writing tools
14. girls' names starting with H
15. squashes

Page 94 Categorizing

wood	Water	Colors
oak	bay	tan
pencil	sea	red
board	pond	blue
forest	lake	green
walnut	river	scarlet
lumber	ocean	beige
maple	creek	chartreuse
Metals	**Space**	**Furniture**
tin	countdown	lamp
iron	Mars	couch
titanium	moon	mirror
aluminum	orbit	chest
steel	astronaut	rocker
copper	weightless	dresser
platinum	rocket	cabinet

Page 95–Page 102
Answers will vary.

Page 103 Number Trivia
1.
144	2
8	1
100	

2. Thailand—Baht   United Kingdom—Pound
Italy—Lira
Japan—Yen   India—Rupee

3. 32 carnations, 20 daisies, 80 flowers altogether
4. United States
5.

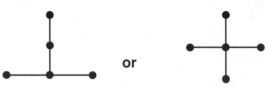 or

Page 104 Rearrange the Numbers
(There are others, but here is one way.)

(1) 8	(2) 6	(3) 5	(4) 10	(5) 6	(6) 11
9	7	4	5	9	5
1	5	9	3	3	2

Page 105 Make Up Your Own
Answers will vary.

Page 106 Vegetable Matters
Answers will vary.

Page 107 Ten-Pin Puzzle
A. 20 B. 14 C. 28 D. 30 E. 32 (highest score possible is 55)

Page 108 Sports Teams
Answers will vary.

Page 109 Triangular Tabulations
27

Page 110-Page 114
Answers will vary.

Page 115 Find the Patterns

91 x 4 = 364	123421	988 x 9 + 4
91 x 5 = 455	1234521	989 x 9 + 3

Page 116 Change the Triangles

Answer Key (cont.)

Page 117 Strike it Rich!
Woodrow Wilson

Page 118 Birthday Parties
1. Victor-May 7
2. Mary-January 1
3. Marco-April 7
4. Christina-February 21
5. Vicky-August 3
6. Mike-October 30
7. Danielle-July 15
8. Peter-March 25

Page 119 Money Maze

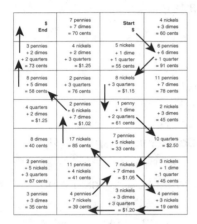

Page 120 Solve These if You Can!
1. $9.65
2. $3.53
3. $2.55
4. $2.65
5. $13.00
6. $27.00

Page 121 What is on the Road?
Answers will vary.

Page 122 and 123 What's in the Bag? #1
1. warm
2. zipper
3. padded
4. camp
5. bed
a sleeping bag

Page 124 and 125 What's in the Bag? #2
1. rectangle
2. fabric
3. wave
4. symbol
5. nation
a flag

Page 126 and 127 What's in the Bag? #3
1. on
2. off
3. portable
4. batteries
5. beam
a flashlight

Page 128 and 129 What's in the Bag? #4
1. mammal
2. arctic
3. swimmer
4. blubber
5. tusks
a walrus

Page 130 Encyclopedias
1. alphabetical
2. dictionary
3. fact
4. entry
5. lexicon
6. volume
7. book
8. topic
9. reference
10. index
11. article
12. thesaurus

Page 131 Kite Safety Rules
Across:
2. storm
6. kite
7. roads
9. tail
10. all
11. trees
Down:
1. power lines
3. bridle
4. open area
5. park
8. safety

Page 132 Cheese Words

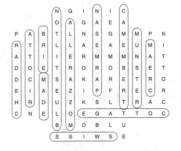

Answer Key (cont.)

Page 133 Hidden Words
sane, shape, shoe, shone, shoo, shop, snap, snoop, soap, soon, span, spoon

Page 134 The Mercedes Wheel
deer, me, red, reed, seed, seem, seemed, cede, creed, deem, seer

Page 135 Solar System Mystery
1. It's the only four-letter name.
2. It's the only name with one vowel.
3. All the other names have a "u," even Earth has "you"!

Page 136 Something Old, Something New
OLD, odd, add, aid, lid, lit, nit, not, net, NEW

Page 137 Inside the Hindenberg
4-letter words: been, bend, bind, bird, deer, dine, ding, Eden, edge, gene, grid, grin, heed, herb, herd, here, hide, hind, hire, need, nerd, nine, reed, rein, ride, rind, ring

5-letter words: begin, beige, being, breed, bride, bring, diner, genie, genre, greed, green, grind, hedge, hinge, hired, inner, neigh, ridge, reign

6-letter words: behind, binder, bridge, dinner, ending, engine, gender, grinned, hinder, hinged, reined

7-letter words: bending, heeding, herding, needing, neighed, reigned

8-letter words: beginner, breeding

Page 138 Spot the Sea Monster
1. squid
2. leviathan
3. shark
4. clam
5. Loch Ness
6. stingray
7. sea-serpent
8. octopus
9. whale
10. kraken

Page 139 End With a Nap!
BED, bet, bat, cat, COT, cop, cap, NAP

Page 140 Bikinis!
maraca, Sahara, banana, Panama, delete, serene, yo-ho-ho, eleven, eyelet

Page 141 Library Find-a-Word
The place where records are kept: Archives

Page 142 It's Not That Easy Being Green
green fly
green bean
Greenland
greenback
greenhouse
green light
green thumb
green pepper
greengrocer
green keeper

Page 143 International Police
German
Dutch
Italian
Spanish
French
Canadian

Page 144 Coats
A coat of paint.

Page 145 More Proverbial Codes
1. Don't count your chickens before they hatch.
2. Birds of a feather flock together.
3. A stitch in time saves nine.
4. A penny saved is a penny earned.
5. Two wrongs don't make a right.
6. Where there is a will, there is a way.
7. Strike while the iron is hot.
8. A watched pot never boils.

Page 146 Frontier Words
1. soddy
2. corn dodgers
3. forty-niners
4. chips
5. emigrants
6. ague
7. rustlers
8. schooner

Answer Key *(cont.)*

Page 147 Palindromes
1. SOS
2. eye
3. mum
4. solos
5. pop
6. wow
7. tot
8. radar
9. gag
10. mom
11. Bob
12. Hannah/Eve
13. madam or ma'am
14. deed
15. ewe

Page 148 Meteorite Mix-Up
tree
trim
eerie
merit
meter
otter
timer
term
remote
termite

Page 149–Page 170
Answers will vary.

Page 171 Math Mystery
The four-digit combination to the briefcase is 5381.

Page 172 Dance Diagrams
Here's one way to explain it:
1. Left foot forward
2. Right foot forward
3. Left foot forward
4. Right foot swings to side
5. Left foot closes to right foot.

Page 173 Investigative Journalist
1. September has only 30 days.
2. Sailboats don't have engines.
3. If they were docked at the pier, the anchor would be down.
4. You can't climb into a full barrel.
5. The barrel becomes a funnel.
6. You can't see tattoos through a black shirt.
7. If it was a fatal shot, how was the story written?

Page 174 On the Farm

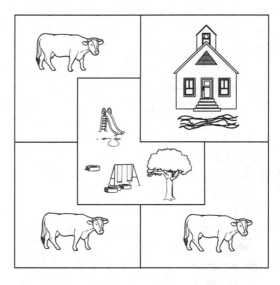

Page 175–Page 187
Answers will vary.

Page 188 Hidden Meanings
1. face to face
2. man overboard
3. split level
4. long underwear
5. deer crossing
6. head over heels
7. business before pleasure
8. order in the court
9. uptown
10. banana split
11. three degrees below zero
12. Minnesota

Answer Key (cont.)

Page 190 Scrambled Math

1. add
2. sum
3. zero
4. half
5. plus
6. minus
7. addition
8. negative
9. digit
10. mathematics
11. subtract
12. times
13. divide
14. fraction
15. number

Page 191 How Many?

1. 12 sides
2. 13 items
3. 5 rings
4. 100 years
5. 13 colonies
6. 5 sides
7. 1 wheel
8. 168 hours
9. 366 days
10. 1,000 years
11. 52 cards
12. 100 centimeters
13. 90 degrees
14. 9 planets
15. 1 eye
16. 88 keys
17. 206 bones
18. 360 degrees
19. 10 events
20. 64 squares

Page 192 Choices

1. You would need to buy more than 10 tacos on special to equal the cost of the t-shirt.
2. It is cheaper to pay 10 cents a mile.

Page 193 Writing Numbers

Arabic	12	13	14	15	16	17	18	19	20
Babylonian	< ▼▼	<▼▼▼	<▼▼▼▼	<▼▼▼▼ ▼▼	<▼▼▼ ▼▼▼	<▼▼▼▼ ▼▼▼	<▼▼▼▼ ▼▼▼▼	<▼▼▼ ▼▼▼ ▼▼▼	<<
Egyptian	Ω II	Ω III	Ω IIII	Ω $\frac{II}{III}$	Ω $\frac{III}{III}$	Ω $\frac{III}{IIII}$	Ω $\frac{IIII}{IIII}$	Ω $\frac{IIII}{IIIII}$	Ω Ω
Roman	XII	XIII	XIV	XV	XVI	XVII	XIII	XIX	XX
Mayan	○○ ══	○○○ ══	○○○○ ══	═══	○ ═══	○○ ═══	○○○ ═══	○○○○ ═══	════
Base 2	1100	1101	1110	1111	10000	10001	10010	10011	10100

Page 194 "Sum" Triangle

a. 2 + 6 + 1 = 9, 1 + 5 + 3 = 9, 3 + 4 + 2 = 9
b. 5 + 4 +1 = 10, 1 + 6 + 3 = 10, 3 + 2 + 5 = 10
c. 6 + 1 + 4 = 11, 4 + 5 + 2 = 11, 2 + 3 + 6 = 11
d. 4 + 2 + 6 = 12, 6 + 1 + 5 = 12, 5 + 3 + 4 = 12

Page 195-Page 196

Answers will vary.

Page 197 Math Names

Ream
Triceratops
Quadruplets
Star of David
Triangle
bicentennial
Bigamy
centurian
decathalon
pentathalon

Page 198 Credit Card Capers

1. contains only even numbers
2. it's a palindrome
3. each four digit number is twice the one before
4. all odd numbers
5. the digits are ordered odd-even-odd-even
6. contains eight two-digit prime numbers
7. double 1 = 2, double 2 = 4, etc.
8. the sum of the first three 4-digit numbers equals the last
9. the sum of the four numbers is 9999
10. when converted to letters of the alphabet they spell credit card (c = 3, r = 18, e = 5, etc.)

Answer Key (cont.)

Page 199

Answers will vary.

Page 200 Consecutive Numbers

1. can't do
2. can't do
3. 1 + 2
4. can't do
5. 2 + 3
6. 1 + 2 + 3
7. 3 + 4
8. can't do
9. 4 + 5 or 2 + 3 + 4
10. 1 + 2 + 3 + 4
11. 5 + 6
12. 3 + 4 + 5
13. 6 + 7
14. 2 + 3 + 4 + 5
15. 7 + 8 or 4 + 5 + 6
16. can't do
17. 8 + 9
18. 3 + 4 + 5 + 6 or 5 + 6 + 7
19. 9 + 10
20. 2 + 3 + 4 + 5 + 6
21. 10 + 11 or 6 + 7 + 8
22. 4 + 5 + 6 + 7
23. 11 + 12
24. 7 + 8 + 9
25. 12 + 13
26. 5 + 6 + 7 + 8
27. 13 + 14 or 8 + 9 + 10
28. 1 + 2 + 3 + 4 + 5 + 6 + 7
29. 14 + 15
30. 6 + 7 + 8 + 9

Page 201 Decimal and Binary Numbers

1. 4
2. 6
3. 9
4. 21
5. 31
6. 10011
7. 111
8. 11001
9. 1010
10. 101

Page 202 Toppling Tree Conundrum

Here's one way: The small trees' shadows (1m) are 1/4 of their height (4m). The tall tree's shadow (5m) must also be 1/4 of its height, which must then be 5 x 4 m = 20 m. Not quite enough room to drop it!

Page 203 Moons of Saturn

Scientist: Christiaan Huygens
Retrograde moon: Phoebe

Page 204-205 What's in the Bag? #5

1. fluffy
2. white
3. sweet
4. tops
5. cocoa

marshmallows

Page 206–207 What's in the Bag? #6

1. lab
2. tool
3. enlarge
4. focus
5. lens

a microscope

Page 208–209 What's in the Bag? #7

1. cooking
2. herb
3. strong
4. white
5. bulb

garlic

Page 210-211 What's in the Bag? #8

1. office
2. tool
3. secures
4. loops
5. wire

a stapler

Page 212 Occupation Word Puzzle

Cellist
Oboist
Musician
Piano tuner
Organist
Soprano
Entertainer
Recorder

Answer Key (cont.)

Page 213 Fast or Slow?
SLOW
slot
slat
flat
fiat
fist
FAST

Page 214 In the Middle
middle age
middle ages
middle C
middle class
middle ear
Middle East
middle man
middle of the road
middle sized
middle weight

Page 215 Totem Poles
1. actual
2. insane
3. defeat
4. train
5. manual
6. escort
7. climb
8. Indian
9. timing
10. horses
11. Reno
12. river
13. plain

Page 216 From Traitor to Patriot
airport
tractor
rattier
apricot
topiary

Page 217 George Giraffe
1. sight
2. seven
3. lion
4. Sahara
5. tongue
6. years
7. migrate
8. acacia
9. brown
10. mammal
11. calf
12. fight
13. herds

Page 218 Zip It Up!
1. chimpanzee
2. citizenship
3. Leipzig
4. marzipan
5. pince nez
6. pizza
7. pizzicato
8. prize
9. puzzling
10. trapezoid
11. zeppelin
12. zip code

Page 219 Bridge Word Search
Chesapeake Bay Bridge Tunnel

Page 220 Jumbo Elephants
1. elephant
2. Asian
3. African
4. mammoth
5. hyena
6. mastodon
7. forage
8. troop
9. mammal
Bonus Word: pachyderm

Answer Key (cont.)

Page 221 Rods

prod

trod

hot rod

piston rod

divining rod

lightning rod

cuisenaire rod

Page 222 Jules Verne Acrostic

1. journey
2. clouds
3. helicopter
4. eighty
5. island
6. movies
7. leagues
8. submarine
9. moon
10. Earth

Page 223 Tammy's Tatoos

hot potato

cottontail

toothpaste

sweet potato

photostat

spotted toad

tree-tomato

Page 224 Tipperary

tape, tarp, tear, tier, tire, trap, tray, trip, type, taper, teary, tripe, tipper, trapper, tripper

Page 225 E's Front and Back

1. execute
2. elevate
3. ease
4. eagle
5. estimate
6. educate
7. envelope
8. evidence
9. exile
10. ewe
11. evacuate
12. examine
13. evaporate
14. exercise
15. encourage
16. executive
17. exhale
18. escape
19. entice
20. emancipate

Page 226 Letter Answers

1. EZ
2. IC
3. CU
4. P
5. C
6. K, D, or B
7. O
8. I
9. U or I
10. TP
11. IV
12. Y
13. T or OJ
14. B
15. DJ

Answer Key (cont.)

Page 227 More Rhyming Word Pairs

1. ill Bill
2. bad lad
3. glum chum
4. shy fly
5. spunky monkey
6. plump ump
7. fluffy puppy
8. sad dad
9. wet pet
10. pink drink
11. steady Teddy
12. sloppy poppy
13. wee flea
14. sick chick
15. sharp harp

Page 228 Word Chains

Answers will vary.

Page 229 Coded Message

1. F
2. O
3. N
4. H
5. A
6. U
7. Y
8. C
9. T
10. K
11. I

famous saying: You can if you think you can.

Page 230–Page 253

Answers will vary.

Page 254 Poem Puzzle

Man Friday

Page 255 Blood Donors

Chris, Scientist, B
Brad, sprinter, A
Alan, secretary, O

Page 256 Hidden Meanings

1. merry-go-round
2. life of ease
3. three blind mice (no i's)
4. ants in your pants
5. all mixed up
6. tricycle
7. I understand
8. cross roads
9. thumbs up
10. once upon a time
11. scrambled eggs
12. just between you and me

Page 257 What is the Question?

Answers will vary.

Page 258 Softball Lineup

Jane 5
Daisy 2
Carrie 9
Joanne 3
Gertie 4
Annie 6
Penny 8
Tammy 1
Lindsey 7

Page 259-Page 280

Answers will vary.

Super Solver Award

To: _____

From: _____

Date: _____

Super Solver Award

To: _____

From: _____

Date: _____

Super Solver Award

To: _____

From: _____

Date: _____

Super Solver Award

To: _____

From: _____

Date: _____